INTERSTELLAR THEME PARK

NEW AND SELECTED WRITING

INTERSTELLAR THEME PARK
NEW AND SELECTED WRITING

JACK SKELLEY

BLAZEVOX[BOOKS]
Buffalo, New York

Interstellar Theme Park
by Jack Skelley
Copyright © 2022

Published by BlazeVOX [books]

Printed in the United States of America

Interior design and typesetting by Geoffrey Gatza
Cover art and inside art: Erin Alexander

First Edition
ISBN: 978-1-60964-411-6
Library of Congress Control Number: 2022937449

BlazeVOX [books]
131 Euclid Ave
Kenmore, NY 14217
Editor@blazevox.org

publisher of weird little books

BlazeVOX [books]

blazevox.org

21 20 19 18 17 16 15 14 13 12 01 02 03 04 05 06 07 08 09 10 11

BlazeVOX

Acknowledgments

Love and gratitude: Dennis Cooper, Amy Gerstler, Benjamin Weissman, David Trinidad, Sabrina Tarasoff, Elaine Equi, Jerome Sala, Kim Rosenfield, Beyond Baroque, Michael Silverblatt. Stephen Spera, Erin Alexander, Robin Carr, Monica Rex, Suzy Marcinek, Dave Childs, Dave Arnson, Sheree Rose, Bill Mohr and The Dark Bob.

Many of these pieces of writing first appeared in the following publications, recordings and other media: Alcatraz, Allium, B City, Barney, Beyond Baroque Magazine, Big Other, Blaze Vox Journal, Bookworm, Brooklyn Review, Coming Attractions, Court Green, Dennis Cooper Blog, Diana's Fourth Almanac, English as a Second Language, Expat, Found Street, Fugitives & Futurists, Harpers, The Hollywood Review, The Illinois Review, Innings and Quarters, Jukebox Terrorists With Typewriters, KXLU, Life of Crime (Black Bart Poetry Society), Little Caesar, Little Product on the Prairie, (mac)ro(mic), Neighborhood Rhythms, Nude Erections, Poetry Loves Poetry, Power Misses: Essays Across (Un)popular Culture, Praxis, Turtle Point, Snap, L.A. Weekly, Los Angeles Contemporary Exhibitions, Santa Monica Review, Sweet Nothings: An Anthology of Rock and Roll in American Poetry, Under 35: The New Generation of American Poets, Unprotected Text, Up Late: American Poetry Since 1970, ZYZZYVA.

Contents

Author's Intro

The writings in this book were produced over four decades. The earliest are from *Monsters*, a 1982 collection on Dennis Cooper's Little Caesar Press. These reflect the explosively creative period and people surrounding Dennis and Beyond Baroque Literary/Arts Center in Venice, where I produced the music series and co-produced the reading and performance series.

This book also includes parts of *Fear of Kathy Acker*, the "secretly legendary" novel composed in the mid-1980s and appearing piecemeal in chapbooks and magazines, but never in its entirety until 2023 from Semiotext(e).

Fast-forward to pandemic daze, with new poems and stories, another creative burst. These two periods – the 80s and the early 2020s – bookend years of additional writing. Much of this was intended for collections entitled *Product Placement* and *Think Tank*. Alas, time and nature are cruel, and those books did not appear. But – Yay! – much of their contents do here.

My first instinct was to arrange *Interstellar Theme Park* in the above chronology. But ever-wise writer and editor Amy Gerstler advised me to re-group it according to motifs. This better reveals its conceptual continuity.

One lifelong, obsessive theme persists: a perverse celebration of pop iconography. It manifests in love/hate liaisons with commodity culture, or elevates to symbology the preposterous yet tenacious expression of the mythic in the personal – the poly-verse of sexual personae that holds and molds our identities. Because mass artifacts are inherently low- middle-brow, I sometimes joke with the coinage "archetypical," as dusty tropes and avatars turn expressive when re-idolized in the everyday.

Induced by music, verging on apotheosis, and rendered in the rituals of sex/romance, branding, Disneyfication and dreams, these icons materialize furthest in cosmology, which is a literary art. An essentially comic one.

In other words, enjoy the rides!

For Lisa, Claire, Bram and Paul

INTERSTELLAR THEME PARK

"If a thing loves, it is infinite." – William Blake

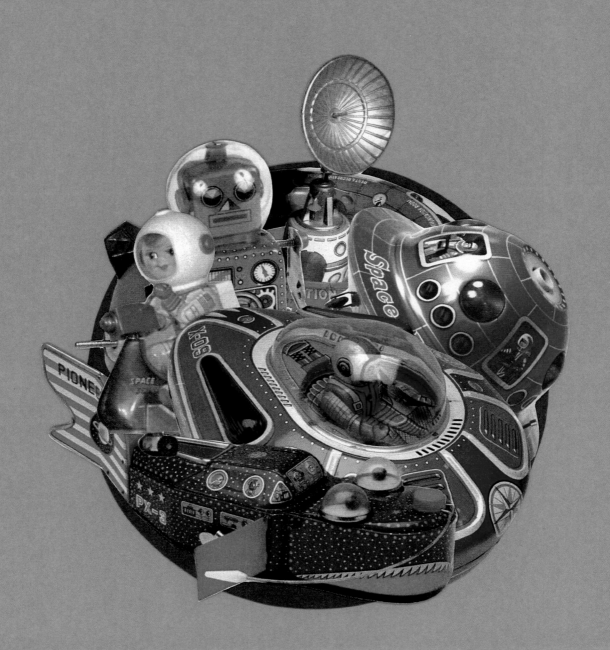

I. Planet of Toys

Interstellar Theme Park

Based on Alejandro Jodorowsky's lost epic, Dune

I want whore-ships
And I want these whore-ships to dock in orbital flesh
I want ruby-throated ornithopters sipping the nectar of dwarf stars
I want Emperor Dali on a toilet throne of dolphins
I want drones that say Yes Daddy
I want H.R. Geiger mausoleums for the 27 Club
I want quasi-suspended animation (genital arousal optional)
I want a planet of toys
I want a jihad of joys
And a gulag of Karens
I want Rimbaudian grammar police
I want woke Stormy Daniels balloon rides
I want light-rail Stations of the Cross
I want Picasso's pajamas 50% off in all emporia
I want Vibrators by Dre standard
I want Syd Barrett-era Pink Floyd to levitate the Tomorrowland Terrace
I want 50-foot Miley Cyrus mourning her Dead Petz on Dog Star Sirius
I want time itself to eddy and unhitch from its turntable of deception
I want Moon Juice cougars – see them jump-start adaptation, anointed with next-gen
    Kardashian lips and hips
I want Fruity Pebbles vaccination bars, with stalactites nippling jelly babies, but
    without the jingle-jangle crash
While we're at it, I want fingers that are 17 trillion light-years long, probing asteroids
    & healing hemorrhoids
I want Aristophanes' tranny-globe beings, rolling around & layered with eyes – day
    and night, without ceasing, they sing
Don't forget: I want on-demand K-holes mouthing the words "now" & "wow,"
    drooling and dripping with *ahegao*
I want rings, blue rings, and rings around rings of Berlin-blue orbs
Get me Stanley Kubrick, I want him to edit all humanity to grunts and symbols

On gas-giant Neptune I want Hello Kitty to be Hell Kitty

I want fresh-baked hosts branded with the Holy Ghost

Oh, and I also want bio-feedback donuts that induce satori

I want 12 Lady Gagas to perform "Lady Madonna" – each one is pregnant and haloed
    with 12 stars

I want drunk-surfing on a river of anti-gravity

And into this river I want a comet called Wormwood to crash with cold fire nightly
    at 9

I want Kali the Destroyer decapitating Parvati from *Survivor*

I want to occupy octopi to learn their language of shape & texture

I want a sunken palace where the spirits of lost lovers murmur

I want thick, chewy anarchy in a candy-colored shell

I want to live-stream Apocalypse Dreams

I want universal chaos

I want the abyss

And, when the Singularity finally arrives, and dumb matter rises to gaze upon itself
    and remember who it always was, I want everyone to defragmentize into their
    star-child, co-mingle dimensions, and upload into each other's arms

Planet of Toys

for Bob Flanagan

When I was frozen the world was warm enough,
I couldn't swim but the seas were still metalized,
no way to go and no where to get to.
Then I requested my first weekend snow rabbit,
and the cranky elders called me forward.
"Steer clear of the southern domes," they intoned,
"Mister Machine keeps the city streets burning,
and will sooner eat you than heat you." But I was uncurious –
I had seen the bushes blaze communing
on my balcony at midnight, and now flew up
to the bluest hangnail moons the mountains touch.
But when Binky clanked dead on me one night
after the power caves were closed,
my only resort was a blood-red pillar
flaming near the black hemisphere.
I was magnetized, of course, long before I set my probes,
or got out the hooks and cables, long
before I landed, or caught the smell the ice makes
when antique cavities are seeping through the cracks,
or heard him hissing always around the next corner;
and by the time I climbed on top of him,
my headlights too clanked closed.
Then, Wammo! What a blast!
Trucks don't pop those balloons,
they're too big, colored bubbles making
worlds multiply, and mind-babies busting out instead—
"The end of all this mechanical foreplay," he concluded;
"No way," I said, "let's get on it again."
I was only fourteen, but I felt ages
of fire pulling up from the gyrations of insurgents

to come; and now I'm warning all you cool girls, yeah,
you'll get wet at the bottom, but it feels good in the summer.

I Lived on a Demon-Sized Planet

'Like what the fuck else we gon do?' – Michelle T. Clinton

It was designed for the smaller but more virulent demons. We found it easy to speed around on little demon scooters, and everyone knew each other's diminutive demon names.

I had a job staging plays with demons and angels. In one play, an elongated demon crushed an angel-sized city with her spike heels. Angry angels ran screaming from tiny buildings.

Best of all were the demon-sized lovers, slim enough to fit inside my demon-sized heart. And yet our emotions were quite large.

Recently, at night, these lovers have returned to me, visiting my regular-sized planet. We re-enact dramas just for each other. Deep in the final scenes, time transmutes into music. One note at a time – out of time – yet smudged together, as lovers smudge with me into one.

Though our planet was small, our emotions never stopped expanding. For a few, unfortunately, the planet became too tiny. They were smudged away.

Love was the biggest emotion. We created the plays to hold our growing feelings. So we could stare at them, and try to understand them.

What the fuck else could we do? Our hearts were too small to hold all that love.

The Caveman Won't Leave You Alone

Based on a line by Roky Erickson

I have always been here before,
Buried in the backyard of my life,
where no Snarol nor Weed-B-Gone can disgorge
the lusty homunculus, root-legged & ash-bearded,
a grubby, G-spot Antifa liberating sunken obelisks.

Like Wagner's excitable sex-dwarf, he mines
vaginal memory, licks his chops over
gems in chasms that can't be spent above ground,
and plows red clay to coin an older currency –
a Golden Age of pantheistic spasms.

Hey, remember when you wormed your way to the topsoil
and projected squirt-porn upon Stonehenge,
flickering like a Playdough allegory?
Oh, how we hopped from top to top of monstrous dominoes
as each wobbled, toppled… then resurrected!

And like Lazarus holed-up in some *laissez-faire* Lascaux,
I won't be lazy when you roll that rock
or jackhammer a vibrator shock. That's how
Lucifer 2.0 freaked the Bejesus out of Betty Rubble,
and raised Pandemonium in reverse gravity.
"Wow, that's underground," we said back then,
tagging trademarks on the walls
of womb-shaped shrines. And man, did we dig it!

With such magic ancestors, you'll never be lonely:
Old Granddad was the Wizard of Ozymandias,
and one grumpy spelunker.

So I tipped his tombstone the night
You and I boozed it up in the boneyard.
Legend has it we enacted necrophilia on a rotting crypt.
"In Memory of Elizabeth Reed," read the engraving.

And those Sea Scrolls down south? They're no more dead,
my dear, than the tongues that roll around your mouth.

Delving through valleys of fecundity,
we tunneled to some mental Ming Dynasty,
where analog edibles dangle, magneted by her ooze.

Now *that* was a cave most moist and delicious!
I shoveled in. My chin glistened.

Hollywood Forever Cemetery Tour Guide

for Karie Bible

Yes, gravestones too,
like the roses around them,
fade, crumble and decay,
even those of "forever" celebrities.
But at least these stars
are privileged with a second life
in the firmament of fame
until the day their last fan dies.

The Gospel of Elon

for Jerome Sala

"There is an ancient tradition of enmity between the fallen angels and Adam, and even more archaic rivalry between good angels and the first man."
--Harold Bloom, *Omens of Millennium*

The original Adam was as large as City Hall.
He wore a garment of emeralds projected
On brushed titanium, with Frank Gehry petals
Peeling like shards of the firmament,
Flowing folds of overpasses, and 80s
Shoulder pads in planetary sizes.
He was born of Barbelo,
The mother-father emanation of pure spirit.
They dispersed fungible funds of energy and equity
To stitch bone, sinew, flesh, marrow,
Blood and skin too vast to fail or many to count.
Striding the earth, he gorged on
orgasms distilled, fetishes fulfilled.

And yet, huge as he was, good-old Adam
Was governed by the Big Guy's
Hand-picked Angels, and the vast
Scope and uncontrollable urges
Of this giant freaked them out with envy.
So they withered Man into his own skin,
Shoved him full of benzos and frizzed
His fiery hair into an undiagnosable rash.

These Angels were Yahweh's yes-men
Who released their stress in the flesh of daughters.
The most pneumatic super-heroines

From Vivid Pictures they would spirit away,
Collared in the celestial bounce-house,
Its blue-tinted dome floated and
Inflated with a clean-burning
Composite of silicone and Cialis.

As cephalopods may assume any color or shape
To communicate, these horndog Seraphim
And Cherubim likewise played X-ray
Games of I-See-What-You-Mean,
Suiting-up in luscious holes and astral
Protuberances, coiling and coupling
Among the stars, alternately
Male, female, both and neither,
Switch-hitting as they pleased.

BTW, from this mating the Angels bred
Their own race of giant sons and daughters.
Young Titans with monstrous appetites,
They devoured all that nurtures growth:
Microprocessors, organic produce, stadia,
Water rights and trade deals.
Still others of these Giants manifested
As athletes. Such Tigers and Serenas
Exceled immeasurably, then reflected,
Meditated, read Deepak and remixed Tupac.
And so doing, they refined their zones of fire
To pure endorsements, and became free.

As for the Angels, they burned up an eternity
Of fat salaries paid in pleasure –
All write-offable but jarred by summoning
To the Top Floor. Here Yahweh, throned
Like a developer behind a desk larger

Than Orange County, his every master-plan
A correction of the one that came before,
Beheld his winged underlings
Nod at every dumb idea.

And so then what happened is,
One fed-up archangel-crat
Cast himself as a rebel in leather,
Cashed-in his F.U. chips and went freelance,
Damning himself to the fickle glory of consulting.

Yes, it was Metatron, the greatest of Angels,
with 36 pairs of wings and eyes immeasurable,
Cleansed by the fervor of direct knowledge of ideas
Into a wizard of names, logos and marks.
A great maker of positioning statements,
A Platonic genie of brands,
A demiurge of urges,
Metatron was also called Enoch,
The Lesser Yahweh, Yaldabaoth
Verizon, Celebrex, Alcatel,
Lucent and 700 other titles.
From ever-compressing lithium-ion
Batteries of racial memory he forged
Fierce emblems, fantasies rampant with
Redundancy and raging metastatically.

And yeah, sure, the Almighty Chairman
Continued to milk his top-down holdings.
But now the angel Metatron
Woke-up the Adam nodding inside,
Thrust awareness back into flesh,
And, no longer constrained by org charts
Or restrictions against eating shellfish,

Jetted among the spheres at will
To reconfigure assets from the
Splinters of heavens within.

So it was he who horizontalized the globe.
It was he who tattooed the nurseries
And rotated his product for the lens
And dictated the cover art
And hallmarked the national parks
And hieroglyphed the inner eyelid
And cornered unborn alphabets
And spiked the formulas
And backward-masked kitchen-table budget talks
And reported web hits to motherships
And cross-promoted in the pews
And confused with fake news
And tapped code on the uterus walls
And scrolled credits in the exit-song of dreams.

He wound-up the start-ups and downgraded the bonds,
Hinged personal wins on mutual ruin,
Raped yearnings with earnings,
Upzoned atmospheres and microwaved glaciers,
Comforted with amnesia and terrorized with memory.

So babies rapped their ABCs in Disney beds,
The Nike swoosh was tongued above each head,
And every mouth remembered what ancient angels said.

Yahweh or the Highway

"I am God. And there are no other gods but Me," he thundered. But if there were no other gods, why was he so damn jealous?

Old Testament Role Reversal

Job's lot was Lot's job

Non-Binary

They say there are
2 kinds of people:
People who divide people
into 2 kinds of people,
and people who don't.

Put me in that group.

Shit-Lit

I invented YOLO, then I got Me-Too'd.

Totalogy

Sometimes fate is inevitable

Doctrine of Plenitude*

I am able to understand my confusion.
I was sitting purposeless, I was distracted
by the dressing of limbs, the parting of lips, I drew
another virile demon or ethereal goddess
from a blank dark: sweat beads on the neck,
down the butt crack, the eyes vacant,
open a slit, a quick gasp, and our biological
priest has mounted his pulpit another time.
And what a majestic pulpit it is! I could
see the gilded ceiling of the cathedral reflecting
beams of light through a part in the curtain. Recalling
that light, I saw there was no need to go
outside of myself. Wanting nothing for use,
needing nothing for replenishment, it was not on account
of desire nor constraint that I ended this black sacrament.

The mind of some great architect might
have conceived ten thousand other possible
worlds than this. But this is the best world
for the purpose that I have in mind. There
is a face I want to see and see. There
are those hips my hands would cup around and lift
and spin. There is my chamber turning past
midnight again, as the walls spin out
and the stars zoom down and the flesh burns up.
The sky is inside this person's skin, clouds
swell warm beneath my fingers and there is
a pullulating stretch under my skull,
a hot series of thoughts—this breathes
ancient light from the planets when they quake on the horizon.
I can diagnose the groans of the biggest

machine. The ocean's growl articulates a song
that I've been humming.

                     I am the sire inseminating
not from urge but momentum. I incorporate
myself worldwide and centralize the bread
and wine: Everyone partakes and everyone is free
beneath me. If I enter us into war without explicit
declaration, I act in our name, just as the infected
blood of father may pass on to a son
with a weakened intellect and will. The law of instinct
determines a rigorous end.

                     I had foreseen
all of this. And when I leave I
shall take with me the spurt of energy
that flung out orbits, threw broad beams
across the vault, installed the lamps and switches.
And when I leave I shall liqudate my conglomerates:
My weapons factories will explode, my reactors
fuse, my drills and tankers will release
their crude. I'll get fed up with myself.
I will want my money back. I
will eat the indistinct elements, and,
in a big flash, body is heaven.

** As traced by historian of ideas Arthur Lovejoy, the Doctrine of Plenitude states that the universe
contains all possible forms of existence.*

Gnostic Remix

Immortality is but ubiquity in time.

She is an infinite realm whose dimensions no angelic generation can see and where the invisible spiritualizes bodies.

In the Gospel of Judas, under the name Nebro (which means rebel), Yaldabaoth engendered Adam and Eve and inadvertently gave humanity fleshly vestiges of the heavens within him, a proprioception* of the divine above.

My Gnostic act of gnosis was the awakening toward awareness of the celestial shards inside.

Who really created Adam?

After God fashioned me out of the earth, along with your mother Eve, I went to bout with others in the glory of the eternal realm we came from. We were superior to the God who gave us shape.

Split into emanations of the spirit above, she lost the knowledge of her own divinity. The inception of corporeal desire is the moment when he and Eve lost the power of eternal knowledge. And become mortal.

The whole population of fleshly beings would wallow in the flood. A Demiurge who lost touch with his heavenly blood.

Proprioception: the awareness of the position and movement of the body.

Smogman Laments His Task

Oh, for a voice like hurricanes, and a tongue to whip
the crawling creatures off the earth, then
I could end this mess. But my influence extends only so far—
so I stretch the webs of smoke above
the cities, even as I snap them striding
through; so I pump the workers' muscles in the mills,
but feed them gaudy paper on the weekend,
bloating them to work it off again;
and so I straggle muttering through the downtown districts
and growling engines of production in the suburbs.

Consumers complain that I was a former Cadillac
dealer, heads of industry that I would regulate
to death, politicians that I was a conservative in an age
of affluence—and I am the biggest man in town!
But still my hands are tied behind me, even
as I hack away at hills behind the bedrooms.
Just feel these hands! These hands were hamburger meat
when I pulled a thousand ropes in shipyards,
these hands dripped cancerous sewage when I rescued drunken
swimmers from the bay, these hands were bloody
stubs when I dug the streets for them to drive on.
Scarred face of bulldozed mountains, flesh corroded
to the bone, skin scaling, itching, burning in a golden bowl of sweat.

I have heard there is a gate of teeth,
which those who pass see as the mouth of a huge
brown monster, ravenous again after their regurgitation.
I have heard that these freeways are his entrails, these fumes
the stuff that gives him gas-pains, these heaped-up steel
constructions burning ulcers in his side.
Well, I have been chewed-up and spat-out for ages

on end, and I have never seen this beast.
But I am bound and blind, and I thrash about
Madly as if in a dream where monkeys poke
At me inside a gunny sack. I know
That if just once someone would wipe these stinging
Poisons from my eyes, I would see
What the outside of this thing looks like, and I would have to grab
One of these smokestacks or TV towers, stab that monster
In the stomach, loosening its gleaming oily guts
And set free forever even those who mock me as I struggle now.

Ekphrastic Movie Reviews

GEORGE BAILEY AS SATAN

He wants to live again:
Not in Bedford Falls,
where he resents his own virtue,
but in his act-three freak-out,
where (finally) he gets to travel…
all the way to a proto Twilight Zone,
jazzed with dancehall skanks,
"Dies Irae" organ swells
and bug-eyed desire.

Weird: Only when he's unborn
is he most defiantly alive.

It's like what Blake says about Milton:
He is of the devil's party without knowing it.

BAD BRAINS*

Expressionoid angles shadow Dr Pretorius,
who grows sexed-up golems with OG alchemy.
But his pupil, Baron von Frankie, plays
Science God instead… with light: "The
glorious ray that breathed life into the world !!!!!"

Works great! But wait: The creature
is diseased and must be appeased.
Too bad Mary Wollstonecraft
left no further instructions.
She was busy inventing Goth.

So the anima is a must as our
degenerate Jungian mate-makers
generate a test-tube hottie
for the malicious hunk to bang.

Dang! If only Fritz hadn't smashed
the "good" cerebellum to bits.
Miscreant minds, like Abby Normal's,
make even worse monsters,

as in "Bad Brain" by The Ramones,
who invented Punk.

*The movies are Bride of Frankenstein and Young Frankenstein (Abby Normal).

ANDY WARHOL'S FRANKENSTEIN

Acker's Law of Archetypes turns Goth to Goof.
By the 70s the Baron has 2 children with his sister,
the kids are Wednesday & Pugsley Addams,
and Igor is Nigel Tufnel from Spinal Tap.

Morrissey (not the Smiths) directs:

- Incel incest
- 3D bolt-ons
- Monstrophilia plus Cronenbergian wound-sex
- Distended bladders
- Führersploitation to a *Lohengrin* loop
- Roma necropolis w/ green-screen Klimt
- A race of Skelter slaves
- Hi-Klass warfare
- ASMR martyrdom
- Whole lotta stigmata
- MacBeth body count

The monster bride is a Factory-fresh Nico-alike,
while Joe Dallesandro sticks to his Brooklynese.

Andy's job was to go to the parties.

TIPPI HEDREN'S TALONS
for David Trinidad

Plague-like and airborne,
"Angry Nature" swarms
to peck and claw civilization
to ruins – but not before
haughty Tippi Hedren
wards-off the harpies
with her blood-red
lacquer tips (and matching
lips), poison-ivy suit,
a Valkyrie helmet of hair,
and about 17 cigarettes.

II. Product Placement

Green Goddess

Who made the salad
Whose tangy vinegar made me wince
Who played pouty Venus to my impudent Caesar
Who taught me to renounce meat
Who flowed forth lubricants
Who performed dark sacraments
Whose tart shrub tangled my tongue
Who with unctuous poses oiled me
Who received my verdant sacrifice
Who, as I reclined panting, poured herself into her dressing
Who lured me to the garden and dragged me into deep greens
Who instructed me on the use of the proper fork
Who inserted an oblong cucumber
Who shredded slender carrot sticks
Whose burning bush consumed the sky god's timbers, shaking his heavens to
    the rafters
Who roused me in damp chambers, dousing reasonable fires to consume
    knowledge raw
Who at the crack of the vernal equinox, broke seasoned bread into bite-sized croutons
Who parted beet-red vestments
Who swelled my painted cave-beast proud and pregnant
Who put me in the red-pepper pink
Whose celestial power I would enviously drink
Who succored me when I lay pallid
Who made the salad

Lemon Pledge

Very pretty and the lemon flower is sweet
In a well-groomed hedge expensive to keep
But a penance well spent on precious waxed wedge
In cunning tribute to twin tributaries' vent
A pagan knight bows to this graven shrine
Racking up calls on a princess Trimline phone
Crotchless and crowned as heels ascend the throne
To kneel before a fist-full of down and marinate the filet
With a twirl of garments she inverts the pyramid
I've been locked inside your heart-shaped box for a week
Polished with Johnson & Johnson to a hard sheen
A lubricated plain landing smoothly on the strip
A sacred cup drained and bitten at the lip
And as the blade must come before the kiss
Her chalice brims with bitter citrus

Crazy Glue

Techno remix unveils the sexual subtext of Saturday night.
I am the councilman officiating the oversized check exchange
Between man's pure horniness and a generosity that exceeds my district.
Wary potential wife, you'd worry harder if I never came over.
I too am looking for the Crazy Glue of commitment.
My detachable face leans into lane changes and a westward view,
A spiral escalator to a downtown loft of estrogen,
Until this cloverleaf moment when my cup runneth on empty
On the stupendous overpass I was just a pane in glass.
But why just Windex myself away and admire the lights,
When I drove from Death Valley to New Year's Eve
To wash up on the Hermosa Beach of your mind, and breathe.

Forgive Me, Botox Jesus

The US Food and Drug Administration (FDA) has approved onabotulinumtoxinA
(Botox) for headache prophylaxis in patients with adult chronic migraine.

Forgive me Botox Jesus.

For the frown lines and the clown eyes that doubted your migraine miracle.

Forgive me Botox Jesus, for I was seduced by the arms and charms of Lady Norco.

Forgive me Botox Jesus, I strayed from the flock, south of your Costco.

For I required the drugs and I desired her hugs.

Forgive me Botox Jesus, for my Norco night nurse – decked in off-white balconette
Wonder Bra push-up padding of timed release and immediate relief –
hardened rounds of rebound headaches. Forgive me, Botox Jesus.

Forgive me, for 10 20 years I fortressed in pills. Forgive me Botox Jesus for they
charmed me but they made me ill.

Forgive me Botox Jesus but the monkeys swarmed me.

Forgive me Botox Jesus, the gummies were good but the CBDs didn't do shit.

Forgive me Botox Jesus, I promise to toothbrush gunk from the porcelain shrine if
only you grant me the detox of barf, lifting the pain of the 'graine that came
from 1990-something, before the advent of your celestial shots.

Forgive me Botox Jesus.

Forgive me Botox Jesus, for while you smoothed the brows of milfs and models, every
Friday without fail the pounding and the electrical nail in the stigmata temple
separated sheep from goats.

Forgive me Botox Jesus, for I countermanded your commandment.

Forgive me Botox Jesus.

I'll flow into your fold and frolic with fluffy lambs on the Final Morning.

Botox Jesus show me your crook.

Oh Botox Jesus promise me my 'graine pain away and I'll stay faithful. I won't stray.

I'll say it: I'll stay.

Forgive me Botox Jesus.

Everything for Baby

Any baby sees a face
where we would see a fish,
that's the baby mind
making faces in a dish,

and baby minds make up the air,
drifting noses into arcs and cones,
all tonal, simultaneous and growing,
growing old and getting cold,

so anybody struck by baby's fish,
once limped and now stiff,
says baby's play is no more fun,
no more baby everyone.

Sack-of-Skin Questionnaire

Do you ever feel that being alive is shockingly bizarre?

Do you scare yourself realizing you're a human consciousness in an animal body? A sack of skin, walking around with other sacks of skin?

If you're speaking before a group, do you freeze and forget what you're saying because it's oh so very strange to live and to think?

Does this unnerve you? Can you bury the anxiety and move on with your day, or does it stop you cold, momentarily paralyze you?

When you're speaking vehemently, do you forget – mid-sentence – what you're so passionate about?

In a conversation, do you get dizzy and hazy-minded zoning-out on someone's animal face?

Do other people notice you doing this?

When you stare at faces, do they look like animals? Like gorillas or dogs?

When you see your own face, do your primate eyes stare back in puzzlement? In disgust?

Does your own species repulse you?

Rather than "attractive" or "unattractive," are human features neutral? Are attributes of physical beauty largely learned responses?

When you're attracted to someone, where does the attraction spring from: You or them? Are you drawn <u>to</u> them, or are you "projecting" your desires <u>onto</u> them?

When you have sex, are you aware that you and your partner are animals? Is that a turn-off or a turn-on? Do you feel foreign in your own body? Does your partner's skin have a metallic taste? When you're fucking, are you inside or outside of yourself?

Why do you feel alienated from your own being?

If you do have these bracing anxieties, what does that say about your mental health?

Does it mean you are "off" in some way? Is this a kind of psychosis?

Do you even have a unique "personality"? Or is that another imposed fiction?

Is it normal to feel that human life is alien to itself?

Is it healthy to question yourself and your perceptions like this, no matter how unnerving or frightening? What if these questions make you unhappy or unstable?

If human consciousness is anxiety-producing and therefore "wrong" or abnormal, then what is right and normal? Is pure dumb matter – a rock or a plant – more "normal" than animal consciousness?

Is the whole world fucked-up, or is it just "you"?

Does all of this make you question your sanity, "happiness" or purpose?

Does it make you suicidal?

I'm Happy Now*

WALKING THROUGH GARDENA WITH A PAINT CAN FULL OF SHIT

Why should I pay the rent
when the landlady won't fix
my toilet and I have to scoop
my own shit into an old paint can,
carry it down the alley
to the laundromat's dumpster
as these middle-class
Japanese-Americans drive by
saying to themselves,
"Oh, there's a nice boy
going to paint his house"?

MY LEG HAIRS TURNED TO GUM

I saw white light flash
over spiders and droopy stalagtites
when my sister Sue's lantern
bumped against my bare legs,
and everyone in the cave,
Jewel Cave, South Dakota,
The longest cave in America,
could hear my echoing scream,
and later asked me why the hair
on my legs had congealed like
wads of chewed-up bubble gum.

I WAS RIDING AN ICE-CREAM TRUCK THROUGH WATTS

I was riding an ice-cream truck
through Watts while training
as a driver/franchiser, when I
and the other trainee had finished
a six-pack and he asked the driver
to stop, who said, "Hell no
I aint stopping," so the other trainee
uplugged the stopper on the floor
of the truck and let go his little
yellow stream right there.

AFTER MY EST WEEKEND

After my EST weekend I wanted
to do everything I never wanted to do,
so first I cleaned up my kitchen, which was
a primordial mess, with 6
bagsfull of green slime in the
refrigerator bottom, and pools
of greasy cockroach larvae stuck
behind the stove, and especially
that roll of old posters under the
sink, which I picked-up
to find many many many
many many many many
cockroaches swarming so
sickeningly I gaped a full 10
seconds before I opened by 3rd-story
window and flung the
fucking thing outside.

PEED UPON BY A PARAPLEGIC

I was content to drink my beer in peace,
but when this bearded guy in a wheelchair
commanded me to help him to the bathroom,
how was I to know he'd force me to struggle
with his zipper while he shivered and sang out,
"Hold my dick! Hold my dick!"
until I finally loosened his pants,
freeing him to squirt all over
my just-washed janitor's uniform?

Stories told to me by Rick Lawndale, Dick Koenig and Bill Morosi.

Di and Isis

Whoa! My decoder ring is translating
moon-babble from distant oval caverns,
and though the breathalizer is over the top,
I walk the line with Ice T and Johnny Cash;
painfully now, they tune to my plea:

Could mandatory air-bags have stemmed
this lemming machete in the sweltering crowd?
Or was planned obsolescence not to be questioned,
coming from the mini-malls, not the beer halls?

And this baby maker, Christ, not
a dozen Dodger Stadiums could
belly her soft-vowel-surnamed progeny,
nor were our tears enough to lubricate
the parched engine of Western Democracy.
It was as if the parasite evolved over eons
to fine-tooth the herd proved overly ardent,
ordering this napalm raid from within.

As for that brown pebble which stuck in her Doc Martins
it had never made a peep, until, roused to sentience,
it cursed my family in the razor-sharp
rap of urban streets, its bitches
and hos choreographed, we now know,
by video directors who trade notes
on who scores more Laker Girls per shoot.

Yin and Yang Cowhides

The best view of today's new beat-the-drum city strides
comes when you plug-in your windshield translatron,
a pure, shatterproof quartz interpreter
that comes in scorched orange or peanut flesh
and instantly wipes clean any residue of spit,
guilt or tainted heritage at the press of plush, touch-tone triggers.

And while you're circling the block looking for sanitized labor,
drive by Eduardo's Cowhide Corner for non-embargoed skins
in Zebra, Peace Sign, Dead Head, Yin and Yang
and many other non-addictive holographic designs.
Zulu spears half-priced this fiscal quarter
with purchase of one fertility icon.

God Raised My Dummy

I killed a puppet when I was still naïve
until steel eyes in the street grates gaped up
let dummy Charlie tell you
they break your neck hard as a dumpster falling
this I learned when a zig-zaggity mouth clamped down

Most of these people you see here are hollow man
as long as they think they're alive
they don't stop talking
But I'll never forget Charlie X
Forgave me my sin against his little head

I just found the hole in the back of his neck
and my fingers snapped his eyelids shut
I could have left him in his underpass
but now there were more dummies than before
and I ran to the cave behind Gower Gulch

Cracked teeth in the clouds splintered
all hail the chief sprawled before Jesus
and Bush is Satan they said rolling together
two balls in a tube zap, like a bolt in the neck
and I smacked the head hard

the sand around his hole was gooey cheese behind Farmer's Market
when their chemicals melt it into clumps
I reached deep inside for Charlie
who longer spoke inside a dummy shell
but tapped my back and shoved out his hands

Red circles glow if you swish your fingers in blood
chamber bowls and the cloudy horses swim in caves

Charlie bolted upright when my jaw dropped and cars on Sunset
rose to heaven like ghosts on a rope
And now I don't pretend I'm separate from you or Charlie

Because I felt hard sockets soften back to life
let this lost and found piece of plastic tell you
God raised Charlie my dummy
I was lazy and sinned on the rusty streets until
God raised my dummy and me to eternal life

City Hall

King Kong, my large but invisible roommate,
hugged the columns atop of City Hall
and waved, just as I turned in my tracks,
fell back-first onto the digital coaster,
and tumbled through old sunny streets.

And where were City Hall police
when Gillespie, the enraged puppeteer,
dragged his victim to the freight
elevator shaft, and dangled her
for hours as he radioed his demands?

Even the most powerful lobbyist,
who hedges his bets in the slums while
painting the beach pastel with bistros,
must tread the corridors of City Hall
in search of Aldo, the shoe-shine man.

It wasn't until I charged into your City Hall
office and broke out in song
that you threw up your hands,
tossed your head back and succumbed
to my steady and inexorable pressure.

Why do I no longer
fly in formation with a dozen
City Halls above the waterfalls
that plunged through my neighborhood,
or among the heaping clouds?

Our Lady of Guadalupe next appeared
not on the side of City Hall, but as the
edifice itself, shedding her veil
like a stone tablet blossoming into
blue stars, and the half-moon as halo.

Juvenile Loitering

Parking in the hills, on the beach, other lonely places with your girlfriend after 10 p.m., inviting the criminal who preys on lovers; following the game, you could go for something to eat; crawling around in the dark, lured by friends until it's too deep, too late—you only seem to utter sounds on another planet.

A safe, well-lit, shallow place satisfies some inquirers; but you've gone and faked more license to fun, tied down all the girlfriends who don't need you, tried to elude inevitable blanks where compulsive angels force images upon dreamers.

You're glad you weren't arrested for curfew last night, even though the guys you were with were caught inside a store a couple hours later. Because parties do not end by 10 p.m. where noise is loudest in the back vault, with rough red and black walls, and cracking sounds pummeling limbs together.

Jarred-apart, 17-year-old Todd told what you are remembering: That one time you and some creep were on acid and ripped off a couple of bicycles and rode them in another opening and all the way down, under Japanese gardeners, rain, dogpiss from all the poodles. The graffiti there said "Red Shit Here 1956," but no shit, too old. You took turns on the girl while the other guy held the flashlight, and you still hear moans in sewer acoustics, see red cracks among broken glass: ants are on the edges, one is crawling on your hand, their blind meandering feels your temple.

And what was just for fun in your a-rhythmic twirls brought that Frankenstein's monster type to throw beer in your face, and that bald-headed boy in a sleeveless T-shirt to dive into your path and send you really spinning.

And what do the girlfriends care now? They spread their own emblems on alley walls, and yank themselves before the best bet, and slip away after the dogs have stopped barking and the traffic dies down, because you guys always crash first and they're wide awake, windows rolled down, doors unlocked.

In the end, the white-winged police will have a few questions for you:

- Are you sure you're of draft age?
- How much do you own of your middle-class heritage?
- Do you really enjoy this so-called music?
- What part of town did you drive from?
- And if somebody drags you home again, or helps you to your feet, finds your keys and points you in the right direction, will you give real thanks, or fall into their arms just for that feeling?

Mockingbird

Strummed against stucco in a yucca staging area
painfully re-circulating earworms & old ideas,
a feathered obnoxoid hurls its blurt
for a riff raid on mandatory amnesia.
He's just horny or hungry but bleats
like Miles one step ahead of the one,
a dialectic simulcast, though the dull brain
perplexes and retards* with waves
that remember yonder amplified chortle.
When a dumb singer absorbs your cathedral guilt
and reels of oboe omens call the tune,
that non-stop fucking mimic just outside your room.

*John Keats, "Ode to a Nightingale"

Death Valley Windowpane

A beer surfer's nervous system flows with foam and splashes the walls of my ribcage, a place that tingles petroglyphs and cacti graffiti crushed against canyons. And, yes, it pours in their limbs like liquid.

Bubbles surface to pop/belch. Through the hourglass a throat gulps waves of starch, flash-flood fizz carves a gulch, and slipknot time funnels powder. Pores are below see-level keyholes to the opposite side of your skin.

Let yourself lounge on pebbles of aqua, peach and purple (you could paint a million mini-malls). Let's make a picnic out of it. Dali's ants can't crawl in smaller trickles than this grid of veins against granite. Here early man stonewashed his jeans and pounded out a message that wavers in a mirage above a hundred-mile-long basement with no outlets.

That's how eddies intimate what the wind articulates when you holler cowabunga at the top of your lungs with Gidget on a thirsty beach. Stomp the ground. That cake cracks as you stretch your toes and she lies naked under a circle sky. You kiss – two animals made of metal.

Now the horizon has got us surrounded, palms pressed against palms and coyotes with palm-tree haircuts who leap, bristle and lick salt like quarts of cooler ice dislodged under all the pressure building up. I farted, and the gas – that gurgling little demon, or tons of them rising from a creek bed, a furnace – fueled explosions up on the sun.

It's hot. Have another beer. It cold-filters all my crooked faults and I tremble like a temblor. Suddenly – or is it slowly? – clouds unfold, muscular with Michelangelo's gods and sun-gold as sung by Joni Mitchell. They are pillowcases dry-cleaned and creased in Egypt, then air-mailed from flats near the Dead Sea.

Jesus' feet felt like this. He showed me his etchings. Acid carved away the crust. This windowpane is clean. Is that my skin or your skin that feels so alien?

For a moment there – really a moment within a moment – I forgot how time works. And so I forgot the moment, and what I was trying to remember. It was very important at the time.

Rosy-fingered panorama lilted her lids and crammed entire epochs into backpacks shouldering geology. It's so quiet here. Until you opened your big fat mouth and burped. When he beds his head on her gurgle stomach, you can feel that distortion edge and echo like Meat Puppets guitars a hundred miles away.

He can't stop laughing. Let it all out: Feel the feelings. The desert is filled with them. A heaving sigh crashed into cul-de-sacs of vegetation – dried and crinkled and returned to dust – then whistled away.

And, yay! Though I stagger, boulder to burning boulder, through the valley of death at a vibratory rate, my flesh fears no flames. For I have an unfair advantage over endless bedrocks laid bare. And shadows roll from the opposite snake hole.

So okay, babe, pop another brew and soothe those blisters. And he loosened his boots in the minutes it took a jet trail to widen and blend with cirrus webs and wisps, five miles high, but like eons ago.

Buggered With a Plantain

That darn Thornbury* next door!
Every time I see him he's either a one-armed woman,
quite young and lovely, with an orange cape
tied around the neck, or else he's that ogre
of a neighbor, all sour and green underneath his smile,
devising how to torture me again.
Today he chopped the heads off my favorite roses
and god how I wanted to squirt him then.
Speaking with him in his own house was useless—his hordes
of teenage daughters were stomping again to the latest
ego-beat, shrieking in a savage chant.
I can't get a word in edgewise! And his stupid
mongrel is forever rubbing a bloody bone
against my leg. And his wife is certainly no help.
All she can do is flutter enormous eyelashes and giggle.
I found myself shaking her violently,
but she just stared right through me
and trembled into different forms: her daughters,
the dog, the strange food in their refrigerator.
And Thorny just sucked his pipe and laughed!
I ran upstairs to beg that goofy son
of theirs for help, and he's there on his bed, surrounded
by dozens of black, one-foot-wide spots,
each one screaming at me: "Go back to the kitchen,
go back, go back, find a fish or piece
of fruit, and ram that sucker up the ass!"
I staggered back downstairs and there
was Thorny, changed into the woman again, face down
on the dinette, a tiny white rump pointing up,
an armless sleeve dangling down,
and all his little girls were painted red
and gathered in a circle. I grabbed a big

green banana, took my aim, and ... God
help me, Harriet, I couldn't control myself!

*Thornbury was the Nelson family's neighbor on sit-com "Ozzie and Harriet."

Plastic Surgery and Your Skin

ONLY DEEP SKIN

When an arm or leg is amputated the phantom limb survives for twenty-one days. A blond-haired boy is born with eyes sinking into wet skin; a woman shines more than moons. Then the stomach stops working and all available blood is flooding the face. When we imagine all the actions are independent textures, the phantom limb persists, a fist forcing the throat, pulsing eyes, lips of scarlet, lakes and craters brimming with desire; and when painted glances draw blood, only deep skin bleeds within.

PERSONALITY FACE

All your life, Duchess, you have been terribly shy and self-conscious because of a tremendous hump in your nose. And although surgery gave you a classic nose, truly beautiful, the magic was not in the scalpel itself. You became bitter and hostile. All the times you tricked me into despair, all your promises and quick escapes—of course, the scar may no longer show, but we can see the hump today—inflict a scar to erase a scar. The German duelists wear theirs proudly, but you can't see the inside of your own skin.

SUCCESSES TO FAILURE

1) Be sensitive to the negative, it can alert us to danger. We recognize something we don't want. Nobody is right disregarding signs along the way. We're going to hang up on everyone who is not hearing anything.

2) The abstract white in the sky for years flashed-out my every idea. But then dense shifting rhythms sang what I would not think. I fought the sound, was overwhelmed, and rose again in anger and accomplishment, standing on a chair, palms waving, arms embracing hellish joy, mind riding on a gush of garble.

3) Everyone knows someone in the family, office or circle of friends who is so thin-skinned that others must continually be on guard lest offence be taken at some passing slight. But you will be too big to feel threatened.

THE PLASTIC TRUTH

The old woman's only arm holds a bloody gauze where her nose would be. Is she drunk? She kicks the window. She wants to point at something. Her fist crumples the gauze before her face. She moves her hand. I clutch the mop-handle: "Oh God!"

Emo Dad

Mammalian instincts concoct life-changing foolishness
with testosterone, dopamine and serotonin,
juicing animal lust into obsessive yearning
and the rituals of romance, all to grease the gears of
attachment and keep the species churning.

This generational trickery continues in the offspring,
who comes out so darn cute he disarms
resentment over sleepless nights and dirty diapers,
and whose resemblance to his parents so flatters their
natural narcissism that they excuse his bad behavior.

And yet, even the most cynical father,
raised on existentialism and punk rock,
feels something somehow more powerful than
hormones and evolution surging through him
when his five-year-old gazes up and says,
"Daddy, can we listen to the Ramones again?"

III.   Artificial Heart

You Make Everything Move Me

Kissing out on the patio.
I drove all night to get here: swish, my pretty breakfast.
You say, hey, I didn't give you any false ideas.
I say I didn't recognize you when I felt this new love.
You are shorter, your hair falls forward.
To the pool then, racing arm in arm.
I sing 'Wild Thing' out loud — it never sounded better.

Disco Paradiso

DANCE FLOOR

Big industry perpetuates a plane
of self-interest, and regulates
for its benefit, not ours.
Presidents throw bullets at random, and smile.
And air-waves tie-up the atmosphere,
wrapping around everything, except
the imagination, which is stacked high
with holy and mysterious things.
Songs and sounds. Your eyes, one
blinks before the other. We're streaming westward
on the mighty 405, slender palms
and aureate smog. You touch my hair
and we wake into this contemporary divine:
The Dodgers have entered the rarified air
of first place. "Dance Floor" by Zapp has supplanted
the Gap Band at number one on the soul charts.
On stage at the Paladium, mystery rhymes
with history as Haircut 100 launches
into a new song. A swimming pool
in the Hollywood hills has a mirrored canopy
so those below may witness swan dives
as from a platform in the sky.
And there are mirrors in your eyes,
where I see what I think are the levels
of Paradise. But as those eyelids shyly blink,
a yonder heaven is starting to unwind,
the visible world reveals its maker
to the creative mind: Everything is really
lumen gloria fashioned from unselfish

love and reflected from within. In other words,
you're the greatest date on earth.
Let's go to the concert and party down.

HEARTBEAT

Let me show you everything in the sky.
The sky is a concrete dome
all crusted over with jewels.
With the clear logic of a dream the dome
opens up – and there I hang.
Only the force-field of reality
holds me between the power of this exterior,
which forgoes the ornaments of romance,
and that interior, which commands me
to go for it. I let go, flopping in my affection,
and plop before you, and you suddenly smile.
Or else you sit in my passenger seat
and sing along with "Heartbeat." Now every
gadget in the city jams up and
I make my confession "Oh, baby,
I really really like you. Pay back
the money I lent you and let's go
to the Planetarium." In the dark
I make my move and your soft pulse is
at my fingertips as we both pretend
to look toward heaven. But there I see
my reverence has crystalized you
into a Diana, and your and everybody's
eyes are red inlaid gems, indistinguishable
as the constellations on spring nights
when you're drunk and you can't find Mars.
I'm drunk and I can't find you.

GENIUS OF LOVE

I see New York in the sky,
from some patio jacuzzi at midnight
as the Tom Tom Club comes on
and everybody's swimming through
their own personal millennium.
But hey, you are cutting
a melodious gyre when you shoot
your blue eyes my way.
I try to keep cool, but
my desire is showing through:
were gonna have some fun.

You and I, we're so mutually jazzed,
it's like we're way jamming
in the world's tightest groove band,
In a ten-tiered disco paradiso,
its empyrean spotlight on the
smartest dancers, instruments
in perfect harmony and sync,
awesome delight flashing over
young faces everywhere.
And by the time were back to my place,
heaven is absolutely happening
for these two bodies that burn in the dark.

Then the whole thing eases into blank
and the worthiness of earth
no longer worries us.
We're traversing planets
with our serene encircling.
We're into the firmament.

And when you finally have to leave, yeah, I'm bummed:
One more corporeal universe has collapsed.
But I know the sky still hangs there in the dark,
though everything else seems to fall apart.

EMERGENCY

It's still dark, my chest is hollow, and aches,
salt tears drop onto my overcooked oatmeal,
then I must go out and meet the masses –
whole shoals of ruined spirits that flop
around my path like grunion, or echo dumb
replies like Chatty Cathies. I want to shout
through the cut-out slot I breathe through,
but I'm drowned out by the shrieking of these corpses
from their burning tombs: Hell's great heresiarchs
compelling us to shrink from our desires.

Yet sometimes, in line for my lunchtime burrito,
I catch sight of two eyes, a nose, the lips
of a pretty saint, who points salaciously toward heaven.
Then I think of you, believe again in miracles.
Maybe I can get you on the phone tonight.

And by the time I'm making dinner, I'm not
so much another big dummy, as a Lazarus
ready to rejoin the living. I have killed
my puppet, that grim traitor, and I autonomously
walk and talk. So I put on a record
and actually dance as the Whispers are moaning, "Operator,
got to talk to her, This is an emergency!"
But when I finally call, no one answers,
Over there it's three hours later.
Where could you be? A big emptiness
begins to gulp me up, and the drift
of burning fish follows from the kitchen.

FORGET ME NOTS

Wow, the blessed virgin has snatched
me to the gate of purgatory itself.
She is this gray-blue flash cube
who burns and vanishes, then twirls
into a woman and proclaims:
"Thou hast reached the edge of heaven
through unselfish love, remember?
Watch out now you don't get lost.
And check it out: Since I am married
to the whole world, die in a thousand teenage
suicide pacts, tote a rifle for every
baby crushed in rubble, a silver half-moon
dangles from my cloudy forehead in the west, see?
I direct all traffic, forward via the past.
But where is your place in Eternity
as long as you nurse your broken heart?
Come, let me take this sleeper."
And she lifts me from my bed
above the cloud cover, amid
a crew of souls, and drops me on the beach,
where I can get a nice tan
and relax listening to my walkman.
And now I wake up hearing "Forget Me Nots"
and really get into it.
I remember you and shiver.
I sure hope you're doing OK.

Makeout Material

For Robin Carr

There's a Santa Ana tonight, so we drive up
Blue Jay Way, and finally I feel like
myself with you. Even after those surfers
gave me a hit of that killer Hawaiian, I
knew I wouldn't get paranoid. From this
vantage everything is so flat and so far: A big
blob of green juts into Orange County
like some sex-urge piercing the left brain,
and a black hole in the middle
of Beverly Hills screams, "Let's eat!"

It's dizzying, that huge twinkly man-made
gunk-pile; but catching you relieved
against such expanse it all seems managable,
miniature, and coming down we make all the lights.
Now, we can go to Red Sea, Delores, Circle Bar,
or anywhere, but somehow we always end up on Pico
and get into some dumb disagreement.
Yes, you're more than makeout material,
but no, we don't have to be commitment city.
I just want to be your friend, give you funny gifts,
write you this poem, and fuck
in that tiny universe we call your bedroom.

...and only I am authorized to bring you into custody

her ankles gathered in prayer
her stations of crossed wrists

her steam-ironed fleece achingly snug
her tendons tangled in a fist

her eyebrows and the skin beside her eyebrows
her two-drink minimum to kiss

her viola restrained in the passenger seat
her shriek for the Captain at midnight

her expertly maintained elastic
her teeth that feel the right decision

her textbook speed and bathroom postcards
her laughter on the fourteenth morning

her Turkish cat and burgandy lager
her Schopenhauer highlight reel

her combustible onramp to glib adultery
her money needed for the carburetor

her pantyless salesmanship at the lemonade stand
her mischievous phone message winking

------

her castle that's dark this time of year
her satellite that's closed for repairs

her manual emotion that slips out of gear
her Ingrid Bergman who smiles, then weeps, then disappears

Hollow Inside

You bite the heads off all the bunnies,
I'll let gloves loose on those yellow peepers,
and together we'll crack every egg
we can find. Then blue light
breaks the blinds and I forget
again who made these echoing calls,
but this Easter morning I'll figure
it out and on the toilet start
by process of elimination:
Now you're not so twinkling and remote, my dear,
that you won't flex your fertility rites,
but you'd rather do than suggest it;
and I never use a wind-up timer—
when the chemicals are cooked I stir and serve them up,
never mind my manners on a midnight bed.
It must have been that other, that polite one,
voicing a desire in my cavernous sleep
he wouldn't dare in the daylight:
Is this year's spring reserved for such feral
prompters, or will I too have a crack
at love in the warm months to come?
Shit! With all this milk chocolate on my hands,
I'll never get a good grip on you.

Pomeranian

Ingrid Bergman's head is the atomic bomb,
language-centered poetry is totally bogus,
Tom Clark got me so stoned I can't think,
everyone around here talks too much,
lips spitting bloody pomegranite seeds,
& then you come along
with these funny blue socks on sexy ankles
but so much give-me-a-break crap to put up with,
being edgy & mumbling w/ yr own outside logic
which really gets to me, like those all-encompassing looks,
but disturbing & sad when you angle yr eyes away,
so devastating & gorgeous
that all this is smashed in my memory.
But what's the point when everything else
is fake or scary, & I care so much I can't sleep,
or eat, & I threw up my orange juice &
stepped in the shit of a little flat-faced dog.
Dang—everything's fucked but you.

Stations of the Cross

I   HE IS CONDEMNED TO DEATH

Each year, in every class, from first to eighth grade, there is one who arouses passion. Jeannie Renardi, Cathy Regaldi, Cheryl Perkins. He creates a list. Who would he kiss. Whose hair softest to stroke. Who best resembles the Tressy doll commercial girl (fantasy crush). And who – with just a look, or something even less sensory – stirs an unknowable ache.

II   HE PICKS UP HIS CROSS

Pressed between the parallel blue plaid sashes of Jeannie Renardi's jumper is her blouse. Beneath this white blouse beats a heart. Pleats play about her knees. White shoes and bare ankles dangle under her desk.

III   HE FALLS FOR THE FIRST TIME

It is decreed: Jeannie Renardi shall be the prettiest. With her straight brown hair and Marilyn beauty mark, Jeannie is queen of the class.

IV   HE ENCOUNTERS HIS HOLY MOTHER

The nuns are covered completely by black habits, except for the white, square slot that windows their faces. The girls' limbs are bare. They stretch from starchy blouses. Tanned shoulders roll underneath. From an adjacent desk he sees freckles and arm hair. Plaid skirts play just above the knees. The girls hike up their skirts when possible, flauting the dress code. He notices.

V   SIMON HELPS HIM CARRY THE CROSS

The girls take recess on a separate playground. They skip rope and pound a rubber ball. Their jumpers twist at their waists. Across the blacktop fly their savage chants and shrieks.

VI   VERONICA WIPES HIS FACE

Cheryl Perkins, with her short bangs, dark eyes and the roundness erupting beneath her jumper, may not be the prettiest. But she lifts a veil somewhere inside him. The geometry between her torso, hair and face reflect a part of himself.

VII   HE FALLS FOR THE SECOND TIME

He looks at the bob of Cheryl Perkins' hair, her black bangs. (Jeannie Renardi, though more "beautiful," has been dethroned.) What is this feeling that crosses scared with elated? That excites yet hurts? His dick fills with blood and drops down salt-and-pepper corduroys. And yet the tingling is light. Inflated. Heavy soft. It's like the sensation he had when he took a plane trip: The vibration plus uplift on the runway.

VIII   HE CONSOLES THE MOTHERS OF JERUSALEM

He reads the word "fuck" on the freeway underpass, and no matter how many times he tells it in confession, he can't erase the nasty word from his thoughts.

IX   HE FALLS FOR THE THIRD TIME

A slow-dance with Loraine Romero is an excuse to press close. Her breasts feel small but certain beneath the fuchsia party dress. A candy wrapper on black heels. Later, when the nuns learn of Mona Geronimo's illicit party, they demand a list of every bad student who attended.

X   HE IS STRIPPED OF HIS GARMENTS

Vicki Getten, a public school girl, takes him into her bathroom and pulls down her panties. He stares at her barely haired wedge but does not touch. Later he is ashamed to tell it in confession.

XI   HE IS NAILED TO THE CROSS

In an after-school game of "tag," on the empty playground, the real object is to touch Cheryl Perkins' boobs. He chases, she suddenly halts, turns to face him, laughs, and lets him to press into her. He feels the roundness. Something urges him. He grips her arms just above both elbows, then holds them behind her back. A captive. Her torso juts forward and there are twin bra straps draping twin clavicles. Still restraining her, he kisses her lips. She relents, then squirms away. Looks back, laughing again. Later that night, because he cannot stop reliving these sensations, he sneaks out. On his bike, he circles her house, anxious to catch her dark hair, dark eyes. This feeling: It burns.

XII   HE ASCENDS AND DIES ON THE CROSS

In the backyard clubhouse, John Pipkin relays what his older brother explained: That when you pee inside a girl's nasty, that's how they have babies. The boys spend whole afternoons detecting bad words in songs: "If I Were a Carpenter" has "would you have my baby," and "Dirty Water" has "...along with lovers, fuckers and thieves." (This is before he discovers Frank Zappa.)

XIII HE IS TAKEN DOWN FROM THE CROSS AND GATHERED IN THE ARMS OF HIS HOLY MOTHER

Even the Beatles or the best songs on Boss Radio are not and never will be in the same realm as the girls. They circle his world like the Blessed Virgin, haloed in blue, atop her crescent moon.

XIV HE IS LAID INTO THE SACRED SEPULCHER

Cheryl Perkins' face framed by her bangs like Snow White, the way they swoop around the dark pools of her eyes, her skirt and thighs, her boobs full beneath her blouse, how they jutted when he pinned her arms, then kissed her… all the features, seen and unseen, never found again but always sought, now and for the rest of life, without end, amen. He writes her name a thousand times on looseleaf.

Saint Theresa of The Valley

Now she reads people into books, and books into angels.

Now her words bless 818 migraines into manuscripts.

Now she telempathies.

Now she heals others when she hurts worse.

Now her quantum equation: Your heartbreak breaks my heart.

Now again she's chased down courtyard paths.

Now she unabashedly bawls her eyes out, a Cahuenga of caring.

Now her sobs consecrate reservoirs.

Now a family of enemies withers & slinks to Laurel Canyons of oblivion.

Now their cruelty makes her radiant.

Now, with wrists pinned and pained, her super-powers grow.

Now she tames abuse into agonized desire.

Now, to trap-door martyrdom and save another victim, she absolves her persecutors.

Now the wounds, once growling teardrop diamonds, stigmata into whispers and unzip
    the skin, taut with tattoos.

Now the scars and the inner scars. The beauty and the inner beauty.

Artificial Heart

THE CAPITAL OF CRAVING

Barney Clark* is dead. Long live the artificial heart. The pipes collapse but the organ plays on. Open his chest and treasure the plastic proof: 112 days of pulmonary spasms.

But who can prove the sustenance of Love in the State?

Where:
-   Financial instruments plasma desire.
-   Credit picks pockets puffed with lust and quotients of cool.
-   Objectification rituals motor the "I wish" and "I want."
-   Corridors teem, then surge with squirts.
-   Blood money courses the corpse of a corpulent corporation.

Meanwhile, you and me? We suck and pump, suck and pump, suck and pump.

ERUPTION AT THE PUMP

Everybody's got to get some action, that surge and squish stuff. Fueled by urges at play
in once-bawling babies, globules of adolescents and clots of
assholes
fuck-ups
slackers
jerks
and flakes
drunk drive the arteries after the game,
they're gonna rear-end you, if you don't swerve…
now!!

So why not rear-end each other, snort each other's crank and shove each other's
lumps? Let's bump fists, slap plump rumps, stab backs, flush lust into sumps, drive to
the dump, and suck up what that Big Pumper and those sucking its butt want us to
want. 'Cause everybody sucks the Big Butt.

People pleasing people pimpin' for profit.

PLASTIC ORGASMS FROM INNER SPACE

The human heart beats itself up
as divas sync lip-filler to
proxy lust for longing in
inner-singer aphrodesia zones,
while your atria palpitate in vain
for a pulse in fuck-me pumps.

At 116 beats per minute the average pop banger pounds faster than a resting heart.
Producer Mark Ronson algorhythms cadences and key changes to stimulate and
simulate with pulsatile
thumping
thrumming
throbbing
in time and tune to prod the systole and diastole of the organ. Through this
contraction and dilation, love object X rises to the occasion.

Fill 'er up!!

And yet, branded as a pump slut,
the over-affection you affected
for your victim/accomplice
came true and filled with real feels.

Drip, drop, the brain pops.

Too hot to trot, the operation
succeeds, but the pain remains
as love surgically sours drama to
trauma, silence to sobs.

Invented in 1980, the Roland 808 Rhythm Composer gave users the power to program parts. Now, in its machine song, medieval romance hardens with kick-attack date-stamps. Its monstrous doom-boom darkens dance-floor chords into dirgy loss and minor-key disaster. The coronometer now must monitor arrhythmic depressions.

You stare at the text. You feel the blow. Faint with a pressure-drop that drains the face, you flinch in horror as blood reverses course, and undergoes throes – erupting with compulsions to atone.

Until, thrashing through blackouts, bedside arias bleed tears: "I'm sorry. I'm so fucking sorry."

MOTOR FUCKER

Like the songs that prod them, your prayers are mechanical. Now you drive into the dump. The dump is the ground of absolutist fictions that dissolve into apologies for ways you fuck each other: The devastation which is the rear-end of desire, that warm fog over the ocean at the start of another summer, the debris of ideas—you drive deep into it.

You are a scholar to the reversals of the heart, the pull of the moon, and the wrack of mighty emotional tides. The heart hurts, it swerves into ruts. The fuel pump runs but is worn and weary, and grumbles on the arterial bypass in the moonlight.

It's dump or be dumped. But where will you find another donor?

As sunlight bleeds, as doom sets, you collapse your calculations, everything you would do to each other. The coronary corollaries you once projected eyeball to eyeball now warble a lovely but lonely
Beep
Beep
Beep.

You slink to the undemanding comfort of the dump. You study the sinking satellite.

* Barney Clark was the first successful human recipient of an artificial heart.

Wilma Flintstone as the Anima

The psyche is founded on a bedrock
of male and female elements
folded within even the most boorish ego.
And the search for the perfect mate
is really the search for the complementing
"other" that resides inside,
within one's evolving soul.
So to furiously propel oneself
through the world in quest of love
is like Fred Flintstone taking off
in his stone-wheeled car after Ann Margrock
his feet spinning in a blur,
making that takata-takata sound,
while the clumsy vehicle is getting nowhere,
when all the time he could be right at home,
happy on his bed of rock, with Wilma.

Phantom Body

I watched you so often
dressing at the mirror
examined you like an x-ray
every turn of torso and face
felt our fingers intertwine
and your shoulders fold into mine
our pulse and breath in sync.

Like a dismembered limb
that lives in memory and pain
I incorporated you
and now your body
is a phantom body
moving through mine
long after you left.

And though it doesn't speak
and dissolves as I reach
through the air
it almost hourly bows my head
presses my chest and throat
until I choke out your name
each time swearing not to again.

IV.   Toxic Assets

Think Tank

At the Think Tank for public memories
talent agents dictate the cover shot

At the Think Tank for collective amnesia
The deluded accuse others of being bought

At the Think Tank for public memories
The wife is rewired and returns clean as usual

At the Think Tank for collective amnesia
we gutted the basement and found a tiny time capsule

At the Think Tank for public memories
the unknowable bailout embraced the firmament

At the Think Tank for collective amnesia
I learned what "collumnated ruins domino" meant

At the Think Tank for public memories
the private sector funneled from dismantled generations

At the Think Tank for collective amnesia
the stand-in mayor cooperated with our investigation

At the Think Tank for public memories
don't stink up the contents of the vat

At the Think Tank for collective amnesia
watch millions more pour into that

Toxic Assets

It wasn't the sub-prime loans on the super-sized homes.
It wasn't the banks that failed or the banks that got bailed.
It wasn't Bear Stearns or the bull market.
It wasn't the flipping or the double-dipping.
It wasn't the 2-hour Ford Expedition commute to the defense plant.
It wasn't 4-hour, Guitar Hero self-medication.
It wasn't 9,000 cellophane-wrapped Christmas baskets.
It wasn't the underwaterfront property.
It wasn't the Starbucks inside the Starbucks inside the Wells Fargo.
It wasn't the MTA or the ATMs.
It wasn't the wars, the whores, or the war-whores.
It wasn't that spritzer from Eliot Spitzer.
It wasn't Jim Cramer without a disclaimer.
It wasn't Joe the Plumber or someone dumber.
It wasn't Bernie Madoff or Rod Blagojevich or any other sonofabitch.
It wasn't a house of cards scattered, and it wasn't lives shattered to shards.
It wasn't "clean coal" or "safe nuclear energy."
It wasn't a carbon Bigfoot.
It wasn't the shoe bomber or the shoe thrower.
It wasn't the Pentagon and it wasn't the Octomom.

It wasn't the implants and it wasn't the sycophants.
It was neither the hedge funds nor the wedge issues.
It wasn't the overnight financing of longtime short-sellers.
It wasn't accounts without accountability, or lying without liability, and it wasn't
      insecure securities.
It wasn't the under-the-counter bonus parties for the over-indulged "counterparties."
It wasn't excessive hemorrhaging from excessive leveraging.
It wasn't the uninsured immigrant at County hospital when gang-green set-in.
It wasn't the Wal-Mart greeter eating his paycheck at Wal-Mart.

It wasn't the wine bars, cheese bars, chocolate bars, olive bars, shampoo bars, or
pedicure bars all immaculately tended at the world's second-largest Whole Foods
in El Segundo.
It wasn't the snout-nosed-garage homes by the last slaughterhouse in the
Inland Empire.
It wasn't the BMWs abandoned in Dubai, or the guest-workers stranded in Dubai.
It wasn't that the malls wouldn't stop multiplying or that the "Real Housewives of
Orange County" were so stultifying.

It wasn't any one thing that was risky, wrong, foolish, painful or ailing.
It's that they were all insured against failing.

'It was the whiteness of the whale
that above all things appalled me.'

Melville's white horror includes:
- Great sharks and pissed-off polar bears.
- Whitecaps and blizzards.
- Zeus as a bleached bull raping Europa.
- Blinding sea-squalls & Coleridge's cursed albatross.
- Vast void of the Milky Way.
- The marble pallor of cadavers, the pale sheets that wrap them, and the shrouded spirits they become.

To these we add KKK robes & white terror.

Appalling, pale, pallid, pallor, ghastly, ghostly, blind, blank, bleach-blond, blanch, milk, *moloko*.

Whale, wallow, white, whirl, wail, veil, vile.

Melville: ...*By its indefiniteness it stabs us from behind with the thought of annihilation.*

The dumb natural world – heartless immensity – is always poised to destroy.

Via fire or fascism.

To white ash.

At Home With the Atom Bomb

History locates us on a dynamic grid.
Here's where the kings are born,
here's where the tanks will roll,
and here's where the work-depleted egos
struggle for a purpose—where hard-boiled
attitudes are the boss, and playful nurturing
copy-kittens are relegated to the
sphere of leisure: he who controls sex
controls society, say the experts, as today's
libidinal references wobble to the brink.

But so abundant in this sickly "flesh-as-possession"
detail, a wrecked and reeling world sets
the stage for a new economy of eros,
cogent strategies redress ideological
and emotional imbalances; the seasons soon
engage, clouds of ignorance dissipate,
and everybody takes the sky — ha, ha, ha—
fiery rages dissolve into azure,
scintillating forms and harmonized surprises,
discovering the flesh of new kinds of friends,
obliterating barriers in lips:
stony preconceptions are destroyed
on April mornings and beautiful old houses
are restored to their original states.

Then suddenly these defeated ids,
after years of being on the outside
looking in, are swept into power,
and their revolution fires the globe.
Populations take the world by the romance
of revolt and humanity becomes the army—today's

terrorist is tomorrow's freedom fighter,
the march of one becomes the history of the other.
Movement in the field thrusts forward
through a spatialized time; accumulations
of struggle are no longer horizontal
but ascending – layer upon layer of reclaimed
apparati populate the state,
so many self-made executives,
now in shiny skyscrapers, passing moral judgment
on indigenous movements in the south.

There they sit in concrete cities,
now imagining the architecture as a fine art,
and those first, fixed, simplest,
most inarticulate manifestations of pure will
are breaking the ground under feet. Soon
the walls themselves are shaking, turn transparent.
These transparent chrome colossi extend into the sky,
a daily black rain from the encroaching north
surrounds and we are frozen in chairs, our
children are frozen in their chairs before
the television, watching a video-purple
mushroom cloud bloom above their last remaining
city. And all the head- and heartaches of moral
ambiguities are resolved as oppression again
descends, and we just close our eyes and relax,
sleep it off for the next few thousand winters.

Reporters Need Sources*

Stress-Free Weddings
Driving While Pregnant
Children's TV

Toy Stories
Sex with Exes
Fear of Flying

Crazy Friends
Play an Instrument
Fantasy Sports Camps

Leaving Computers On
Office Relationships
Research in Motion

Adult Bullies
Domestic Violence
Beer Distribution

Anxiety and Depression
Homeless in Winter
Life Insurance

Cappuccino
Handkerchiefs
Jukeboxes

Presidential Speechwriters
Battle Gear
Prehistoric Carnivores

Sexual Stereotypes
One-Night Stands
Treating Night Terrors

Birth Control
Adult Halloween Activities
The Secrets of Love

Actual requests for experts from journalist service ProfNet

First Lady

Eyelash elixir from an iconic distillery
We could get married on your and my salary
Your clump of bean sprouts, my stalk of celery
Want hot new pumps? Just send the bill to me
A place to frame faces, a hair-media gallery
Thick glints of adornment, blinded by jewelry
Hats off to her who needs no millinery
Whom the radical right endeavored to pillory
Increasing domestic from cuts in the military
A campaign coif of practical filigree
Out of the darkess he groped for the will to be
Ritual serpent-squashing, once a millenary
At the end of the century all changed, changed utterly
My eyes popped open when before I'd squint miserably

Reagan Is An Old Fart

Reagan is an Old Fart.
Reagan is a stinky oily fart
seeping out the anus of an old corpulent
Boss masturbating in the Dark.
Reagan is the fart and everyone
smells it every day. Reagan is a Mirror
of a Monkey's Butt and the Sky is
a sandwich bag of Reagan's Meat.
Reagan's Meat is big toes
and Baby Heads, accumulating in the Air,
a shower of ears, hard petals on our hair.
We can't steer the car
and we run right over the Baby.
When the lid comes down at Night
we think about the news of the Day—
Everybody's Brains blasted open.
Reagan is an old sterile Baby Smasher,
a rock bottom dollar Druid,
a quivering Pharoah drowning on the Air,
a stinky old Scab in the Sky.
Some big gaudy Phenomenon
got your Mama to come along, and
Big Monkey Butt got Big Government
off her Back and down her Throat fast.
Bagged her in the Bathroom, broke her Back,
the Backbone of America, her great
Breadbasket Bank made from scratch,
bum raps, hard breaks—she sank in Thick Fog
last Night at Sea, stuffed in a sack,
past the Graveyard of Lost Lifeguard Towers
and Mobsters and Dogs in the Marketplace.
Get a load of those Dragon's Jaws,

everybody, not just bad breath,
but a big fat Dragon, hooting and howling
in his Flames, humping with his spurs on,
his flacid Prick flapping, fucking
and farting, the fucking old Fart Ass.
Smother his Ass of a Face, one last taste of
his foul Gas, he'll swallow it and fall,
we could all kick him out of this Space,
it stank after he came, got uptight, set up
shop, wagered Lives in the Workplace, wrought
his Remedy, and remade Memory like Baby Brains –
audacious on the face of it – he staged a coup Man,
in your Mind – Why do you think you
don't think so good no more, dude? The old
Pruneface shrank your Thinking, a limp Dick
hung it out to dry, Dead Weight, impeach from
the Brain, it stank after he came, and
everyone succumbed. Just a few still smell
his Oily Fart Air, the Oil in his Hair, those
who aren't numb and those who aren't Dead.
If you know, you care. Reagan is an
Old Fart. Heave him out your Head.

V. Athena Del Rey

To Marie Osmond

for Amy Gerstler

There you are again,
your crystal-perfect lace
on the cover of the Enquirer.
It seems you're everywhere this spring,
on more magazines than April has roses.
And yes, your series flopped, but you really are
more suited to the slit sequined dresses of NBC
than to Family Circle declarations of virginity.
Lips of a TV Venus should pucker, not pout.

And what a waste that the nine men you love,
hinted at in this week's Star, turn out
to be your father and eight brothers, that
the husband you dream of would be another perfect virgin.
Your daddy's Mormon domain is as barren
of life as his head is of hair; let me be your conquering
consort and you'll be a far richer heiress, when
the shadows of Utah's long Winter are fled,
and you stand alone on the Rockies, surveying
an ancient city of soft buildings, which transubstantiate
and interpenetrate in moon-aluminum evening, where warm
headlighted insects dance in circles, and golden
movie star men stand upright among beasts,
holding tokens of serpents, sunglasses, electric guitars.

Put aside your moral raiment and I
alone among them come forth to offer
a litany of ardor: my bride, my guide, my lady,
my baby, couch of wisdom, crystal meth
connection, green plastic garden pail,

ice-covered pencil sharpener,
brand-new house in white-hot flames,
bright-painted gate to beautiful things,
interlocking dancer's thighs of black diamonds,
mystical video disk unfolding precisely
like flowers, tree-lined La Cienega to Hollywood
in autumn, angel of the air, arriving
in clean reception, woman made of cities,
Intricately busy with her own construction.

Once we were the issue of chaos, Marie, asleep
In the snows of virtue; now we wake up to mutual delight,
As priests and presidents wither into indefinite night.

Twice as Many Gorillas

for Ava Gardner

Now listen here, Guinevere, one more shot
like that and you're inside the lizard noose,
I'll string you up with the iguana, or ship
you to a convent—see if you can get
the cleric's collar off your neck when you're
frazzled, spooked, and all played out.
No more midnight swims with your two handy men
and beach boy lancelots, Misters Urge and Purge.
Admit it baby, you begin your nightly
scenes with traces of a noble Spanish accent,
but soon you've dropped it altogether, sometimes
snarling a remark in Spanish slang, trotting
around the animal compound in high heels.
And by the end you're a dancing barefoot contessa,
your fingernails just exuding peals
of take-me/forsake-me polish, as your curls and earrings
and black satin skirt make shakey orbits
around the one salacious plea your eyes
can offer. You have a plan for every
sleeping purpose: to rouse it until another
victim comes slinking back, expecting
some damage in the dark and then some rest.
Yes, I know the businessman master planner
made us all monkeys' uncles with our urges,
but you have twice as many gorillas
bounding through your supposedly civilized brain,
and you can't soothe them 'till they break the bars,
make a big mess, and cower back inside again.

Athena Del Rey
California Names New Pandemic Avatar

FOR IMMEDIATE RELEASE
VENICE, Ca -- **United CityStates of California** (UCC)
Homeland Secretary **Miley Cyrus** announced today the appointment of **Lana Del Rey** as new **Chief Avatar** of **Pandemic Defense**. Del Rey, founder of **Venice Bisch**, the "goddess co-op" launched last year, replaces retiring Avatar **Vanna White**. The new position includes a new name for the Avatar department: **Tyche**.

"Tyche is no **Wheel of Fortune** but a **Wheel of Destiny**," sang Cyrus. "**Flood, Drought, Fire, Quake** – and yes, **Virus** – obey our tutelary spirit, **Queen Califia**. We hail Lana Del Rey, and trust our **Health** not to chance, but to destiny!"

Avatar branding is also new. Created by **Artemisia Gentileschi**, the Tyche bureau's Wheel of Fortune logo now depicts **Queen Califia** holding:
- **A Cornucopia**: Spilling serpents, sunglasses, skateboards.
- **A Gubernaculum**: Ship rudder on whale-watching craft.
- **Tarot Cards**: A collaboration between poet **Elaine Equi** and artist **Jules Muck**. (The deck includes a portrait of **Dr. Anthony Fauci**.)

Designed by architect **Zaha Hadid**, the Queen's crown is fashioned as a citadel woven with Sativa leaves.

Del Rey reports directly to UCC Co-Presidents **Nicki Minaj, Ariana Grande, Dua Lipa, Exene & Grimes**.

Autotune Vagina Vortex

They had matching cowboy hats. The bride was Starr.

My Yukon holds 8 but there were 12 or more, overlapping each other's laps. I was yelling, "Easy, girls," recalling my daughter's bachelorette party. But these girls are whooping and don't hear nothing. I slot my phone and turn on reverse video. More fun for them. More tip for me.

That did it. Next thing Starr's spreading her legs wide and pushing her snatch up to the camera. Right up in it as I drive.

"Go, Uber Granny, go!"

So then they ALL pull up their gowns and yank off their panties. Red and royal blue and turquoise gowns, satin shiny, high-slit and single-shouldered goddess gowns. Each is flopping, grappling to push their prize pussies to the camera. Proud. Then the boobs. Thrusting waving pouting and Starr in the center shrieks & hoots above them all.

SATIN RAINBOW TUNNEL

I knew I shouldn't have taken the tunnel. Too late: Missed the exit. But now it's not normal tunnel. Not TNT-blasted rock, but Rainbow Tunnel of Satin lined with girl gowns. Soft-serve sherbet swirl shined and pasteled in flutters. The world's greatest garment maker or artist Christo hypnotizing & smoothing the tube in moss green and rose-gold turquoise pink.

(I stay focused on the road!!!)

And the girls rock my Yukon. I keep us moving, laughing, singing.

All this time, the Sirius radio is skipping in and out of channels. I normally keep it on Classic Rewind or Chill. But it's flying through every one of them for a couple seconds each: the rap, the soul, country, metal, Christian, sports, Howard Stern.
But then the radio channels one voice: a deep warble, or 2 or 3 voices joined. Like autotuned singers who don't sing but talk inside the music. A speaking spirit.

You came from me. You come to me.

I don't dare touch the radio. Because now **I KNOW THAT VOICE.** I've heard it before and will never forget it:

In Sedona with Gidget at vernal Equinox we off-roaded the pink Jeep to Bell Rock to stargaze and it's midnight and we're holding hands flat on our backs in the perfect **POWER VORTEX** at the top center of the rock: That's a **PERFECT** circle in the center of a **CIRCULAR VALLEY,** when clouds fluttered open and cracked a crimson gash, with the moon like a shiny clit-pierce pearl. Vagina sky, ringed by stars. And the voice said,

> *You came and you come from me*
> *Center circle is where you go*
> *Over and through and under you*
> *A daughter and another mother*

Gidget heard it too. "That voice is sound en-souled. Aristotle defined it," she said. "These voices channel signs of affection equal for all. And we hear the spirit of the Mother Star."

MAGNIFICATION OF ORGASMIFICATION

In the tunnel with the bridesmaids, the pink and green fades. A channel of satin walls turns to ruby red membrane. Surging lapping rippling and slipping. It's dripping like Kartchner Caverns.

(I have my wipers on full!)

Tunnel skin grips the estrogen-messy Yukon and muscles it forward as the girls shriek spasms and grab snatches.

Then the autotune vortex sings:
Love flesh flowed in flood
Souled in blood
Morning and Evening Star
The bride gash gush splash squirts
And the puddle mirrors stars.

And Yukon slides & shimmies through tunnel lustered by orgasm ripples.
The Mother Father
Whose Name is not named,
Who came from the heights of Fullness,
Light of Star of the realms of Light,
Light of the silence of Forethought
Father Light of Silence,
Mother Light of Word
Daughter Light of the Incorruptions,
Infinite Light and radiance from the realms of Light
of the unrevealed, undisclosed,
Unaging Mother of Sisters circling rivers of light
Aeon of aeons before and ever more
self-generated, self-generating,
self-producing, truly true eternal realms of the heights of light

I felt it. I know Starr felt it and all the bridesmaids felt it. The shudder spasm channel, the tunnel of light and soul flesh.

And you know what? I have the video. I recorded the whole thing. It's dark because it was the tunnel. But you can hear the song!

You wanna hear it?

Alien Sex on "Wheel of Fortune"

I've assembled my dinner. *Burritos de champiñones.* I turn on the TV and chew. "Wheel of Fortune" glows into focus. There's Vanna White in Grecian gown. The camera zooms. Even her laugh-lines are glamorous.

But something is off. There are no synthesizer crescendos, no cheezy theme song, no sound at all—even as Vanna's lips move. White teeth beaming, covered and uncovered by her painted mouth. The effect is mesmerizing: off/on semaphore sparkle smile, diamond drip dangled between boobs, crystaline eyes flitting under black lashes and flanked by drop earrings: All flash and play, sans sound.

I check the volume control.

The living room lights go out. Everything but the TV screen. The camera circles Vanna, a boxed Athena beckoning with broad product-display gestures. Pan to the Wheel of Fortune, its colors saturate and spin against spiral galaxies.

The Wheel circles. A 3-D mandala elevates the room. Colors splash stucco walls. I can follow one color-panel and revolve with it, or center on the Wheel and its magnetism.

This is better than "Jeopardy."

Finally I hear a voice. It's Pat Sajak. Firmly, confidently, Pat Sajak tells truths in revolving video color.

"We are now transported by strand particle waves that flow through all matter, all time, all souls," states Pat. "Your eyes are not funnels which suck-in 'outside' light. They are rather tunnels pouring images through Consciousness. You create a Vortex of Translucence in every direction you gaze. And yet, beyond perception, you enter a state of Knowledge. Hieroglyph opera. Behold your Tech-Telepathy: This is how you hear me now. Dazed by a neophysics which subverts the clockwork universe, you apprehend a spacecraft bodied by organs of thought, shimmered one-by-one into corporeality. These creatures are known as Aliens."

Shit. Should I turn off the TV? No go. I can only sit and stare.

"We go now to the ancient Sumarian throneroom..." continues Pat Sajak, my interior pilot. "This is the vault of the Sky-God who orders the heavens. At the helm – the control center of a Vessel which mutates at will, a mammoth, conscious, fleshy, space-borne organism – sits Ergotonium, god of incipient teleologies. On his right sits our goddess Vanna, mute oracle. And on his left, Kanye, high and talking in tongues. Arrayed behind is the pantheon of hyper-evolved beings: Choose one— they appear!"

OK. I'll go along with that. I summon silicone porn goddess Danielle Derek. Lately she's been on my mind.

And there she poses, in sun-gold monikini, pointed heels.

"Come here, Daddy," she coos. "I open my holes to you. And you open your Soul to Danielle's resin, a potion flowing in Himalayas of lust. Peer into my folds of walls to see the consummation of your species. In adolescence, it was self-absorbed in auto-erotic ego-body. But as you surge in post-terrestrial communion, a Metafuture of Love, unhindered, expands. This fusion births Transformation. Come, and enter Apocalypses of Possibilities!"

Clothed in the sun, Danielle kneels on leopard-skin pillow. With blinged fingers spreads vagina, and opens mouth into O. Oh oh oh. I force my eyes open when I press into her. Sexual fulfillment helixes like DNA: All possible futures are engaged as senses pull through layers of Language. Thousands of stories and one story. Infinite images and one image, circling, circling. The wisdom of ages palpably surrounds. intercourse is Logos. Sexual communion with aliens is transdimensional transport.

A Handi-Wipes commercial comes on.

Jealous Monsters

THE ABDOMINAL SNOWMAN

...who hangs around my building between midnight
and 6 a.m., demanding money: "Gimme
a quarter. How about a penny? A penny?!?!"
Tonight he woke me up again. "You _do_
have vermin in your kitchen, and carpet moths
which crumble in your fingers. Tomorrow night
I rip your girlfriends pants off!" In the morning
I have an upset stomach, but I know
someone who will nurse me back to health.

MACHINE-BEING IN HIS DEN

...who rants and raves at bears and skulls and birds.
He's awfully scary with those purple
eyes and whirling metal fists; he burns craters
where he walks, and can grind you up good.
But catch him at home and he's docile enough.
The bears are pink baby decals, the skulls
are bought from Mexican liquor stores
in October, and the little hen is dead.

PAC-MAN

...who is not monster, but a little yellow
dot who runs through mazes swallowing monsters.
These turn blue out of envy and float ghost-like
to their tiny square after-life. After winning three games
Pac-Man grows a bit, does a little gobbling dance,
and the player gets one free game credit. One young
Pac-Man champion, after winning 300 game credits, could
not hold his huge expanding Pac-Man on the screen.
This Pac-Man devoured 5 video game parlors, 10 liquor
stores, and 14 Bank of Americas before the Air Force
crushed him on his way to Las Vegas.

A MAN AND NOT A MAN

...who paints a goddess on the ceiling of his imagination.
She becomes a hag in the sky
who points accusing fingers. He runs
in terror through the city, but the streets
are full of her servants, civil monsters
with beaks and uniforms, who stomp into the night,
blasting every man in sight. Soon he joins
their ranks, and feels a rush of pleasure
as he jabs his gun into the air.

VI.   Disneyland

Disneyland

MAINSTREET USA

Ragtime music comes out of
little green speakers in the trees
as one of the Three Little Pigs
is dryhumping a girl in shorts.

FANTASYLAND

Please keep your hands and arms
inside your teacup while your
teacup is in motion.

FRONTIERLAND

My tongue in your mouth
your hand in my pants.
Injun Joe's Cave.

ADVENTURELAND

I'm buying a tiki necklace
while the big cement treehouse
pumps out its incessant
oomba oomba oomba oomba
oomba oomba oomba oomba

TOMORROWLAND

Let the stage rise from the ground
let the beautiful green flowers
pull up in the sky
and let the cheezy top 40 band
play Prince's immortal "1999."

7 Deaths at Disneyland

1. Matterhorn Beheading (standing up for a low overhang)

2. Crushed in the Wheels of America Sings (attendant dies to "Yankee Doodle")

3. Stabbing in Fantasyland (assailant was apprehended in Frontierland)

4. and 5. Double Bucket Dump (couple leans too far in the Skyway to Tomorrowland)

6. Heart Attack (slow to order an ambulance, park officials protected the fantasy atmosphere)

7. Drowning in the Rivers of America (this "Grad Night" fatality was a dark waterway collision)

Disneyland Dreams

The Gulf War is still raging. I walk to the entrance of Disneyland, but a burly Marine tells me I can't come in without a yellow ribbon.

At Disneyland, I pass between two new rides. I explain that the large fans are used to direct the loudspeaker sound effects in the correct direction and also to deflect any extraneous sounds. This, I remember, is similar to Gurdieff/Ousspenksy's* theme of audio "buffers," which drape a barrage of sound in the air to prevent us from remembering ourselves.

We are walking through a Disneyland/college campus. Many women lie there attempting to lure men. In Tomorrowland I am seized with a desire to ride the adventures in Frontierland and Fantasyland. I suggest this and everyone follows me in a new direction. Disneyland becomes a maze of houses and streets. Some houses look antique or Western, so I figure I'm on the right track, but we somehow find ourselves outside of the park. Someone says, "This is the end of Sunset Boulevard." So I reverse direction, searching for the center of the park, but I can't find it. Ultimately, the city gives way to rugged natural terrain and we come to the edge of the continent and a large, churning ocean. I press on, up the coast, up the cliffs, while my comrades stay behind in a gentle valley, under a makeshift shelter. "Look at what we made," they say. I find myself facing a series of trials: I must climb up a sandy cliff but it's too slippery and the roots and branches slip and break in my hand. I am reminded of a night terror from my childhood in which dead branches became live snakes in my fists. I plunge upward, grabbing at anything until I am forced to surrender to fate. I let go. I fall and fall and finally stop, not into the ocean but onto a narrow sandy ledge. I walk around the side of the hill I was trying to ascend and see a sewer opening, or some gaping concrete structure. "Oh, this is how to do it: Go around and under," I realize. How simple. But then I see a shadow in this cave-like structure and it turns out to be a large, angry dog. I must subdue the beast with my bare hands. Again I surrender blindly to the task, and wrestle it without thinking. Soon the dog is simply under my control. I meet up with my companions and we proceed to a large and ornate dome of Arabian pastries and toys.

In a Disneyland dark ride, the cars are on a long, narrow train. The track curves very slowly, unlike most rides. Indoors, through vast rooms, it passes backlit landscapes, bright with Impressionist fogs. An invisible and wise woman is telling the story: We had asked to become Hobbits and this was our home. But an evil witch has threatened us with a brilliant red vision of herself, a glowing ball above our heads. This scarlet witch ball resembles the beating-heart nucleus of the atom in Monsanto Adventure Thru Inner Space. We feel the presence of our bodiless narrator, her voice ringing above, as she guides our car past the red witch ball and the train increases speed down a steep grade. I sit in the very front. At the climax of the ride are sharp jerks in the track which send echoes of screams all the way to the rear of the train. I can see the switches on the track coming. I am facing sideways and in danger of falling off but the car finally coasts through a hidden door. The cave walls are painted in giant splashes of blue and green and the Hobbits sing a happy song.

Lisa and I have a fight before I go to Disneyland. When I get there, Disneyland is closed. I'm stranded at the gate, and no one comes to pick me up.

We are walking through Disneyland when Lisa informs me that she is pregnant. I want to ride the Haunted Mansion because it has new "doom buggies" that fly. But I can't because Disneyland is filled to capacity.

I am on the Matterhorn ride, chugging up the dark tunnel to the top of the mountain. When I get to the top I know that the ride is supposed to take me outside and allow me to fly around Disneyland. But when I get to the top I slide back to the bottom again. This happens several times and is quite frustrating until... the banana between my legs suddenly inflates! Aha: If I simply relax and let the banana carry me, I can float away from the Matterhorn. I reach the top, let go, and continue to ascend as my banana lifts me outside the cave and around the park. I can fly in any direction I please. And only now is the park – once a confounding maze – laid out like a mandala map below me to reveal its secrets.

* Gurdieff/Ousspenksy: Pyotr Demianovich Ouspenskii was a Russian esotericist known for his expositions of the early work of the Greek–Armenian teacher of esoteric doctrine George Gurdjieff. Their concept of "self-remembering" is consisent with the Buddhist practice of mindfulness.

Helium Kid in Space Mountain*

for Sabrina Tarasoff

I had the whole car to myself,
blazing to the bone, science fiction city,
screaming my head off through comets and clusters
and the 2-D doughnut that rolls around,
until, taking that last turn speeding down
through total black to hit a thousand white
explosions, my car jerked still,
all lights frozen and this pimply
employee with a flashlight and cap was saying
stay in your seat and no flashes when I knew another
car was speeding down the track to smash
mine if I didn't say OK and get moving,
closing my eyes hard to bring on the black
and opening them again to the dark wind.

It's an unrhymed sonnet.

Goofy's Bounce House

Goofy burst in sputtering, thrusting his garden shears high.

"Duhh, OK, now who's pooped in my petoonias?"

Mickey's Toontown was overrun with Melrose brats, baggy-pants mini gang-bangers, and grungies. The mollied-out pimple teens first drifted over from Videopolis. Now every snotty alterna-kid in the country partied in Toontown. Goofy had had it up to his snout.

There was the Beverly Hills Brenda look-alike who blew skag and nodded in the bathroom by Toontown Jolly Trolley depot. The toons had to hop over her body to take their break. And Mickey stubbed his bulbous shoes on her Doc Martins.

Then there was that grunge queen in hip huggers, red pendleton and Dr. Seuss hat, with Pearl Jam ghetto blasting on Gadget's Go-Coaster. She spent an afternoon with one ear pressed to the ride speaker's mechanical squawk, her other ear on her rock woofers. 13 coaster trips later, she staggered from her acorn car and barfed all over Chip and Dale.

And every day there surged MTV gangsta kids flopping in the phattest hoodies, more like cartoon trolls than Toontown's actual toons. There they slumped, markers and spray cans in hands, snagging their baggy sleeves on the pottery at Minnie's House and tagging the Jolly Trolley.

Toontown was open just a few weeks and already looked more like Pacoima than Disneyland.

But... when Goofy walked around his Bounce House, following a trampled path through his prize petoonias to find a shit pile in his favorite flowers, well, this was more than the toon could take.

"OK. That's it! Duh, hey, you, c'mere!"

He yanked the first kid he saw by the hood, and shoved his shears through the nostrils, snipping and slicing into nasal passages. They poked through the back of the skull like Roger Rabbit's ears. Goofy's clippers wobbled until he yanked them out. He left a gloppy snotty twerp sputtering blood on the ground.

He turned to his next victim, a toddler in Ren and Stimpy baseball jacket.

"Duh, hey, no non-Disney product allowed!" His puffy white gloves fit tight around the girl's neck. It took longer to strangle her than if she were an actual toon, he thought. Her eyes rolled to tiny white planets then wobbled back into sockets.

Now Goofy spotted Miss Grunge Princess 1993 with her Eddy Vedder fetish. The flannelette flayed her purple hair and dropped her music box as she saw Goofy lunge, his gloves soaked with blood, pawing the air.

"Duh. Hey, this ain't no Seattle. This is Toontown! See?" Goofy snagged her Sony and bashed her brains.

He whipped off her studded belt and wrapped the girl's wrists behind her. He grabbed a clump of purple mane and stuffed it in her mouth. He yanked down her pre-torn jeans and giant boxers. And with his trusty scissors, he sliced through her flannel shirt, snapped open her black bra and pulled off the rest of her clothes. She was bound squirming on the floor of Goofy's Bounce House.

"Guyuk, guyuk, the flannel is flyin' now!" he yelped as he pounced on her and mooshed her face into the round furniture.

"Duuuuuh, grunge, grunge, grunge, grunge.
If I lived in Seattle I'd wear flannel.
I'd work in Grungyland.
I'd be horny for Californy.
Grind my corn cob in Moosehead barns.

Snow and totems, Audrey Horne, and Chris Cornell. Woo, woo woo, drunken Indian summer, and safe in the storm. Nothin' could be warmer than Courtney Love's grinder. Alice in Wonderland Chains on the brains.
Who's yer master, miss disaster?
Change yer channel but don't change yer flannel!
Change yer channel but don't change yer flannel!"

And when the Toontown police finally arrived, though Goofy had since quieted to a blubbery blob, he yanked down the chandelier as he was arrested.

He hurled it on the heads of three more kids before he was carried away.

VII.   Rawk!

Don't Worry Baby

As Mozart's *Marriage of Figaro* wedded
excruciating eloquence with dusty plots,
so Brian Wilson carved from California car songs
the most sublime 2:11 of the 60s,
all the more expressive for its awkward union
of perfect melody and lame lyric:
"I guess I should have kept my mouth shut
when I'd start to brag about my car."

Brian Jones

for Dennis Cooper

MISTER SHAMPOO

"It's going to happen, I tell you," Brian lisped insistently. "It's going to happen soon." Then he turned away from Mick and Keith. Brian slipped a shilling into the meter which turned on the gas fire – a few precious minutes of heat – and shook his wet hair over it.

Mick was in another of his this-isn't-working-out-and-I-should-return-to-accounting-school moods. Yes, since Brian got the group together last year he had booked a trickle of gigs around London. But the only attention the Rolling Stones were getting came from the "jazz snobs," as Brian called them, or from the mods, rockers and art students whose bloody rows usually got the shows closed anyway. And now it was winter, the worst winter in 100 years. And Brian and Mick and Keith were crowded in a piss-cold, two-room flat with a single light bulb that hung Bohemian-style from the ceiling.

Mick was standing under it now, in a periwinkle ladies housecoat.

"I mean we've only played one show this month, Brian," he said. "And we still haven't got paid for that. It just doesn't add up, does it?"

But Brian wasn't worried. Keith's guitar parts were starting to kick in. And they had a great new version of "Not Fade Away" that didn't so much toughen Buddy Holly's hit as demoralize it. Keith imposed a Bo Diddley stomp over it, while Mick snarled his commands and Brian slurped mocking asides on harp. What's more, Brian was on the verge of closing a management deal with Andrew Loog Oldham. Brian hated Loog; he was just a cheeky publicist looking to get rich off the blues. But as the Stones' manager he could get them more gigs. And he could get Brian an extra five pounds a month salary. Five pounds his flatmates didn't have to know about.

A shilling's worth of gas spent, Brian began his brushing. One hundred strokes will catch the blokes, he remembers his mother once said. And Brian's blond mop was glazed to a sheen.

Mick was still bitching.

"I mean what do you think?" he turned to Keith.

Keith was in a cross-legged pose, plunking on Brian's Gibson, his fingers stiff with cold. Brian finished brushing, then smoothed his new tab-collar shirt in the loo mirror.

"I'd like to know who filched my piece of chicken," said Keith.

Too late. Brian was already out the door.

Mick crossed his arms and glared, first at Keith, who shrugged and returned to riffing, then at the door as it slammed shut. He heard Brian bound down the stairs. "Mister Shampoo!" Mick sneered. "And where did he get that shilling?"

THE BLACK BEETLES, THE BLOND MEDUSA

It was in Munich that Brian met Anita. It had been a rough show – there's always some crazy Kraut who throws a beer stein at the stage. Brian barely dodged one and it got him a bit twitchy. And afterwards Mick and Keith were baiting Brian again as he hunched in a corner of the dressing room.

"What's the matter, Brian? Did you see the black beetles again?" Mick laughed. Then Keith laughed, and so Loog laughed. And they all laughed.

"The black beetles, ha ha ha."

Huge swarms of black beetles were what Brian had hallucinated coming out of the wall at Keith's house back in London. And Mick and Keith always seemed to bring up Brian's bad trip just when he felt the most vulnerable to their taunts.

But now someone stopped them in their tracks.

"Hello. Who's this rare bird?" said Mick.

There she was. Anita Pallenberg. An aristocratic beauty, with hair the exact color of Brian's. She even wore a floppy hat and French jacket similar to his. Able to slink past roadies and promoters with the stony gaze of a model, Anita arrived backstage and homed-in not on Mick or Keith, but on Brian.

"I said, who's this?' Mick repeated. But Anita cut him off with a scowl. She sidled next to Brian and, between her fishnets, flashed him a glimpse of her hash and amyl nitrite.

That night, Anita took Brian to her bed. She put on *Aftermath*.

"It's my favorite. I've completely worn out the grooves," she said.

He boffed her, burying himself in her limbs, her hair. Then he cried in her arms… partly in joy, partly in relief, because now he sensed a way out. He pictured her wicked mane gleaming through the window of his Silver Cloud Rolls as it swooped through London. They would be magazine demigods, and Mick would envy every glossy spread, and every journalist's rave for how Brian's sitar fired up "Paint It Black," or how his flute forged a magical Elizabethan blues on "Ruby Tuesday." Best of all, Mick would be stuck with Chrissie Shrimpton – that stupid girl, the mere *sister* of a model – while Brian would have this empress of decadence, this Teutonic Medusa.

Anita drifted into sleep.

Brian whispered, "I need you."

On the turntable the needle clicked, clicked, clicked.

THE BENTLEY

Keith's Bentley purred as it swerved around a herd of goats. An old Frenchman made a rude gesture, but inside all you could hear was Tom, their Cockney chauffeur, yapping about his paratroop days. Brian and Anita were on holiday with Keith, motoring from Paris to Tangier, which had become the Stones' sanctuary ever since London's police were hounding them.

Though Anita nestled with him in the back seat, and his asthma medication was never out of reach, Brian's anxiety was rising with each kilometer.

By now the Stones' social life was a game of superstar chess. Outclassed by Anita, Mick had dumped Chrissie Shrimpton with a vengeance, swooping up Marianne Faithful, whose pale hair and pedigree rivaled Anita's. This made Keith, still lacking a socialite girlfriend, the odd Stone out. So he renewed his bond with Brian who was relieved to have Keith back in his camp. But what were Keith's real intentions? And why were Keith and Anita glancing at each other?

By the time they reached Toulon, Brian was wheezing severely. Anita felt his forehead.

"Brian, you're burning up! Tom, find a hospital!"

Brian was admitted, and though she offered to stay with him, something made Brian urge Anita to continue south with the others. That night, while Brian writhed in a French clinic, Keith and Anita were screwing in a Spanish hotel.

For three days Brian fired off message after panicked message, all of which went ignored until the Bentley arrived in Tangier. By the time he rejoined the Stones' party, which now included Mick, Marianne, and a whole entourage, Brian was certain something was up between Anita and Keith.

The others could sense it too. Tension was thick on the 10th floor of Tangier's Hotel El Minzah, and the all-night acid parties only made things weirder. Brian balled himself into a corner, a Scotch and Coke glued to his fist, and watched. By the time the party got rowdy – Tom the chauffeur tobogganing down the hallway on room-service carts – Brian had crept into town by himself. He returned to his and Anita's suite with a local prostitute – ornate tattoos were burned into her neck and cheeks – and he insisted on a ménage à trois. But Anita was not in the mood.

Then came the barrage.

"You fucking bitch!" he screamed. He picked up a platter of couscous and Frisbee'd it at Anita's head.

The beatings and the cries went on into the night and were heard down the hall, clearly bumming everyone's trip.

In the afternoon, Anita appeared on the patio, her face caked with foundation and concealer. Keith bobbed in the pool before Anita and she stared back, a mixture of passion and pleading.

A few tables over, Mick whispered to Marianne, "Things are getting fuckin' heavy around here. Somebody's got to do something about Brian."

And so Brian was escorted to the central square to record Moroccan music, and when he returned to the hotel the desk clerk gave him the news: Keith had thrown Anita into his Bentley and driven off hours ago. The entire Stones entourage had flown back to London without even telling him.

Brian raced up to his room.

"Judas!" he screamed, and flung a potted plant out the window.

FRINGE

The children flocked around Brian who was seated on a donkey as he entered the ancient village of Jajouka.

"See the man with the big hair! See the man with the big hair!" They trailed him, showering him with fig leaves.

The artist Brion Gysin was taking Brian and Brian's new girlfriend Suki – the latest stand-in for Anita Pallenberg – into the remote Rif mountains of Morocco to document the pre-Islamic rites of Pan.

Brian squatted with the master musicians of Jajouka, smoked from their pipes, picked up their instruments and began wailing, just as he did back in '62 when he learned to play the blues harp in one day. He played along with them a bit more, then supervised the recording. Headphones pressed to his ears, he stalked around the musicians, whirling the microphone in arcs and figure-eights, swaying with the twining of the pipes. Brian knew that one day the rest of the world, too, would purify itself in these waves of sound.

Then, towards dawn, the Jajoukans prepared the sacrifice. An elder in a white kaftan carried a goat the color of desert sand to a flat rock. Brian fixated on this goat. The animal stared back through its shaggy fringe.

The blade swooped down and the scream ripped through the air.

"That's me," choked Brian. "That's me."

INHALER

It has only been a month since Mick, Keith and Charlie drove out to Brian's farm, offering him 100,000 pounds to leave the Rolling Stones.

After the meeting, Brian laid his head on the table and wept. But now, on the night of July 2, Brian is relaxing, watching *Doctor in the House* on the BBC with three friends.

It's been a warm week, the pollen count is high and Brian hits his asthma inhaler between shots of brandy. After the program, Brian takes his guests outside for a swim. He staggers on the diving board, but Brian is a good swimmer and slices through the deep end. After 11 p.m., one by one, all three of Brian's guests remove themselves to the house.

Brian swims alone.

It's a watery blues that Brian hears now. A frantic alto sax gurgles bop from a muddy delta. There it yoo-hoos on sitar, soars above the hills of Wales, then plunges to the mountains of Jajouka, where African reed instruments, the texture of raised tattoos, bleat like goats with circular breathing, gasp infinity, then smudge away in the smoke. Twin Renaissance recorders harmonize bitterly but resolve to a plunked marimba. Deep down in the mix, a blues harp heaves, trailing clouds of echo.

And a metal tube slithers on steel strings, falling down frets to the bottom of the scale, where – bump, by bump, by bony bump – at last it settles, with a perfect twang.

Led Zeppelin

ROBERT PLANT

July 1977, Led Zeppelin is on its eleventh and final American tour. Singer Robert Plant is sitting in his room in the Royal Orleans Hotel. He has just hung up the telephone after talking for two hours with his wife at Jennings Farm, England. He has learned that his son, Karac, has died of a mysterious virus. He leans back on the bed, pulls tightly on his long blond hair, and moans.

Woe to the delusions of men whose lives have known extremes. And curses on beguiling gods, who smile and poison children in their sleep.

I named him Karac, for the Celtic hero Caractacus, son of Cymbeline, who waged against the Romans on the shores of Britain. Caractacus was captured and enslaved, but for his valor Claudius spared his life.

Oh, that some emperor or god had spared my innocent boy.

Once I called myself a golden god, standing on the shores of England, looking Westward, to America, the land we were to conquer. Greater than Jesus or the Beatles, we puffed with pride, demanded tribute from adoring masses, and wagered with wicked forces for record grosses.

Now I pity a man who claims superstar omnipotence.

How unhappy, how utterly alone he is. For while he struts before his millions, or sleeps surrounded by groupie flocks, a dark intruder slips into his home, and wrecks his family, the only thing he never had to fight for, but counted as a gift from God.

Is this now the curse the tabloids blame, the price of our unnatural fame? Is disaster the result of Jimmy's dabbling in occult? No, let them go. Just one suspended me so far to fall so low: my faulty self, who left his family fatherless in the wilds of Jennings Farm.

But now when I sing, I hear above me, in the clouds, shrill winds descending from the hills of Wales, singing of evil and infection in Albion's fertile womb. Woe to him who will not hear my song of doom.

BONZO

As soon as they lifted off from New Orleans, Bonzo lumbered down the aisle to the tour plane's fully stocked bar and began downing screwdriver after screwdriver. He hung onto his personal roadie, Mick, and cried about how he missed his wife and daughter. Fat tears flowed through his thick beard and dropped in his drink.

"That's alright, Bonzo," said Mick. "We'll be home in a few weeks."

But this frustrated Bonzo all the more, and he hurled his empty glass to the front of the plane. It happened to smack a reporter from Sounds on the shoulder. He turned in mock annoyance, not knowing it was Bonzo, and called, "Hey, what's this? Who heaved this drink at me?"

Now a cloud passed over Bonzo's face as he recognized the reporter. Led Zeppelin had been getting bad reviews since the beginning of their career—mostly from snotty snobby critics who disapproved of the band's primal appeal to American kids and who discounted their loftier musical aspirations.

All Bonzo's rage boiled up. He was just a sincere drummer who longed for his wife to hold him again, not some heavy wooden hack, out to screw himself to death. But this is how the world saw John Bonham. And it was all the fault of writers like this one.

His face reddened. He sputtered.

"I've taken enough shit from you cunts in the press!" and he lunged towards the journalist. It took 3 others to pry Bonzo off the man, soothe him and stuff him into a seat. There he drank some more until he passed out and wet his pants.

He was jolted awake when the jet landed in Dallas Fort Worth. He squinted out the window. The red and gray carcass of an armadillo or something was flattened out on the runway near the plane. A buzzard landed there and craned its neck. It seemed to look right at Bonzo.

JOHN PAUL JONES

I don't mind being in the background. I wouldn't like to be out front playing like Jimmy. I believe you should do what you have to do, and if I'm bass, rather than try to lead on bass and push myself, I prefer to put down a good solid line.

However, I did have a lot of songwriting influence on our latest album, *Presence*. And I enjoy the shaping and molding of our sound, if not playing all the parts. We've always been a very architectural, or architectonic, rock band, really, with Bonzo and me laying a heavy frame, and Robert and Jimmy flying upwards, like towers, with buttresses. Kind of a rock and roll Notre Dame, you might say. Actually, Notre Dame was the first Rock and Roll cathedral, many people don't realize this. But we did, of course, and our music even has this same spiritualism.

So what I envisioned for a song such as "Achilles Last Stand" was a sort of rocking monument to heroism and emotion, with Jimmy's harmonized guitars forming colonnades like, to Robert's epic, um, pronouncement, you might say. I believe we're definitely in our Hellenistic period with this song.

You see, Led Zeppelin can change from being a Greek Temple, to a Gothic Cathedral as I said, to a mythical "Stairway to Heaven," eh? . . . to the hardest rockiest cave funk that you'll ever hear.

Architects invented rock 'n' roll really. They're the first rockers because they move rocks. This is a theory I'll be giving more thought to.

Did you know that Mozart invented reggae?

JIMMY PAGE

He walked to the balcony of the Edgewater Inn and looked over Puget Sound. The clouds broke and splayed an aureate sun into cryptic rays. Jimmy was suddenly homesick—not for England, but for L.A., its golden smog, and for the little yellow Christmas lights that framed the bar at the Rainbow. . . and for Lori.

He felt the silver pentagram he picked out for Lori's 16th birthday. He remembered her hard pointed breasts, how they barely relented in to his cupped hands when she lay stretched on the bed at the Hyatt House. But how her buttocks were soft as a baby's, and remained so even after many spanks and whippings. And how then she would turn around and moan for him, "I want to get you hot and hard. Fuck me, baby, fuck me with your big cock. Oh, I'll do anything you say. . . oh!"

And all the women he'd had, they all melted into a confusion of desire and obligation. All except Lori. She stood out clear and pure. She loved him without any demands.

"She's an angel." he sighed, and walked inside to hit up again.

That night on stage, "Dazed and Confused" dissolved into "Whole Lotta Love," and Jimmy conjured monstrous whale cries and sonorous echoes from down inside. He was diving to Atlantis, or the depths of Mordor, as blue green light shifted and shimmered via the new lasers and fog machines. And he was at the center of the light, relaying it with his mirrored guitar across the wide stadium, where it spiraled up to the highest seats.

Then, like a god whose seed is wasted on his own creation, he felt empty. He had emitted all his long soaring blues lines. He gazed in stillness across a teeming bowl of adulation.

For one brief moment, swaying in a liquid space, amidst that sea of shaggy headed stoners, he envisioned Lori's face.

Dennis Wilson and Charlie Manson

SEXY SADIE

Summer 1968. 14400 Sunset Boulevard, Pacific Palisades.

His toes are 10 inches long. Baby snakes squirming on shag carpet. Pulsing. Thickening. Pulsing.

What the fuck is he wearing? His green cashmere sweater is somehow the sleeves of a robe. Oh, yeah: The girls had ripped up his closet and sewn loose garments for the entire "Family." His robe, too, purrs and pulses with squiggle-snakes. Their tiny eyes return his stare.

"Whoa! Buckle-up, loadie," he tells himself.

Dennis is peaking. Peaking hard. But cool. Who could have a bad trip here? He leases a big Craftsman cabin in the canyon. The place glows with golden vibes. The swimming pool is shaped like the state of California, for Christ's sake.

He melts into the massive chair.

"Here. It's 125 mics of pure Owsley," Charlie told him earlier. "You'll get full-on ego-death, man."

This is going to be an all-nighter. Better put on the brakes just in case.

"Sadie, baby, Get your ass in here," he growls. "I want a screwdriver. And where's the hash I got you guys?"

Of the dozen or so girls living in Dennis' home, Sadie most joined hotness with indulgence: Eyes big, doll-like, demi-lidded. Mane dark, silken even when unwashed. Body of a stripper… which is what she was pre-Charlie. She came with a repertoire of pervy delights, eager to escalate his every fetish.

Sadie bounces in from the patio, trailing auras, her flower-priestess kaftan hemmed high.

She genuflects with drink, *plus* bottle, *plus* hash pipe, curls at his feet and gazes up. Despite the heavy dose and the blowjobs earlier, Dennis is hard again and godhead horny.

"Put your head in Daddy's lap." A command. He downs the drink.

"Dennis, Charlie says we don't have crushes." Sadie is teasing. "Everyone shares. Charlie will start orgy porgy when other girls get back."

"Hush. Make that fucking skank face for me. I'm using it. Now." He smacks the pout, fists a knot of hair, and commences pumping mouth.

More than music, booze and drugs, Dennis Wilson loved women. Or more accurately, the *attention* of women – ever since his Hawthorne Middle School Top 10 Bitchen Girls lists.

You'd say he craved adulation if it weren't so easy to get. The only Beach Boy who surfed, his sunny face was a California dream. He got laid way more than brothers Brian and Carl. (Definitely more than obnoxious cousin Mike.) And now it was 1968. All he had to do was pilot his Mercedes through the endless tide of hippie chicks.

That's how he had netted Patricia and Ella Jo on PCH two months ago, taking them home for a three-way. It was through them he met the scrawny freak: Coming back from the studio that night, the log cabin lights were blazing and a school bus blocked the driveway.

"You gonna hurt me?" Dennis had asked. The little man got down on his knees and kissed Dennis' feet.

"Do I look like I'm gonna hurt you?" He had a twang.

"Dennis, this is Charlie! Our guru who I told you about," said one of the girls. "He's a holy man!"

Dennis found the house and pool burbling with nymphs. One by one, they too kneeled and kissed his feet.

"I love you, Dennis."

"I love you, Dennis!"

"Dennis, I love you so much!"

Into the summer his house, food, cars and clothes went to Charlie. In return, the surf-satyr frolicked at will with narcodelic naiads.

Everyone was a freak these days. This weird-ass talked racist Jesus shit about black people. Apocalypse prophesies. But when Dennis was high – when wasn't he? – the Charlie rants poured like mystic party talk. Plus Charlie had songs. And Brother Records, the Beach Boys' new label, needed fresh talent, not more nostalgia.

…But right now Dennis needs Sadie…

"Wh, wh, wh, WHOA! FUUUUUCK!"

Load blows, synapses singe, everything goes goopy. Reflections off the pool ripple with force into the room.

> *Aqua to black.*
>
> *A cymbal crash in reverse, from whisper to smash.*
>
> *Waves of breath.*
>
> *A rubber sun plops into water, dripping red.*
>
> *Bubbling…. Gasping…. gurgling….*
>
> *Come in, closer, closer, closer…*

"Please don't tell Charlie, okay, Dennis?"

There is Sadie's face: beatific/sloppy.

"Wait. What?"

"He won't be happy."

"Huh? …. Oh. So what. I'm not afraid of that little creep. Where's the lighter? Let's do that hash."

APPLE PAN
Fall 1968. 10452 Bellagio Road, Bel Air.

"Brian, we got burgers!"

Silence.

"Come down, Bri. I went to Apple Pan… Hey, also the Wizard is here!"

Dennis plops three bags stuffed with hamburgers and fries on Brian's dining room table.

More silence. Just the wall-to-wall buzz of Brian's TV.

By 1968 the Beach Boys' mojo (including chart prowess) had sunk. Dennis was their image, but Brian was their essence. He composed the material. He produced the records, re-inventing the studio along the way. He built the *concept* of the concept album, the product of anxious/admiring pissing matches with McCartney and The Beatles.

It was all forged in a crucible of pain.

Brian was driven to de-haunt his innocence from the fucked-up torments of their dad Murry –

- who boxed Brian's head till it bled, making his right ear permanently deaf,

- who screamed, "You pussy!" when Brian flinched, then bashed him again,
- who hit Dennis even harder,
- who forced Brian to shit on a newspaper in the kitchen,
- who popped-out his glass eye and made the boys peer into the hideous hole,
- who, even after their adult success, fraudulently sold their catalog, Sea of Tunes, worth a fortune, for a measly sum because the songs were "outdated."

And so, yearning for love and to wave-length with God, Brian, the oldest, the most fragile of all three brothers, tried LSD one night in 1965.

It shattered him.

Sure, that morning at his piano Brian had shimmered out the modulating intro to "California Girls," then the entire song in one day. Then *Pet Sounds*, a suite of bittersweet chamber-pop laced with acid influence, then *Smile*, a majestic cut-up monument, weaving deeper than the Beatles could dream, but cast before a world that wanted car songs… and left unfinished. Brian spun out of orbit and stopped writing. Dennis was different. Egocide was a joy ride. Even the odd bum-out – like the time he lost the ability to form thoughts, and his face cratered in the bathroom mirror – always snapped back to goof/blast: Surfing this moment – no *this* moment – as it fractured and splayed.

But Brian and his demons were a slow-motion crash, with the audio hallucinations on endless repeat – dear old Dad yelling in his dead ear.

So here he is, slumped in bed. 300 pounds. Zoning on coke and dexies to daytime reruns.

The hamburgers are to lure him to the studio – easy ransom for a kidnapped muse.

"No, Dennis! I'm sleeping! Go home!" Brian moans.

"But Brian, I brought the Wizard…"

Dennis looks at Charlie, fidgeting, pacing the whole time. (The girls a mute bouquet.)

"So is Terry coming? He said he'd listen," snarls Charlie.

Terry Melcher was the big producer friend of the Beach Boys. Dennis had been prodding Terry to audition "The Wizard" – Dennis' name for Charlie – as some kind of musical genius.

Brian upstairs: "Keep him out of here. That guy stinks up the studio!"

Charlie: "Call Terry, Dennis. Call him now. He said he'd get me the record deal. And *you* said you'd pay me for my songs. You *owe* me, man!"

"Charlie, you smashed my Ferrari and you've been crashing in my home for half a year. I don't owe you shit!"

Brian: "I'm trying to concentrate! Be quiet! It hurts!"

Charlie: "I heard what you did with my song, Dennis. With 'Cease to Exist.' You changed the words. Don't deny it!"

Charlie extracts his oversized switchblade. Looks at Dennis dead-on. Tosses the knife hand to hand. Still staring. Scrapes dirt from his fingernails. (Which is funny because his hands were always grimy.)

"Maybe today was a bad idea, Charlie. Maybe this was *all* a bad idea."

Eyes lock. Time freezes. The only sound is upstairs:
> *The Professor and MaryAnn!*
> *Here on Gilligan's Isle!*

"Let's go, girls," Charlie finally says.

"But Charlie!" one of them demurs, "Dennis drove us."

"Stand back and stand by! Get the food!"

Beady pupils pin Dennis: "We know where to find Terry Melcher. And we definitely know where to find YOU!"

They grab the burger bags and slam the door, shaking Brian's home.

Eventually Brian lumbers down in robe and slippers. His bloodshot eyes blear right past his brother… who stares into some internal abyss.

"I thought you went to Apple Pan. Where's the burgers?"

RISE

Spring, 1969. 10050 Cielo Drive, Benedict Canyon.

Five months before the murders, Charlie speaks to Rudy Altobelli, owner of the home Terry Melcher had leased, now housing Roman Polanski and Sharon Tate.

I am called Jesus, I am called the Buddha, I am called Big Boolabog.
I was a stranger and you did not invite me in.

Dennis Dummy Wilson took me here with Terry Piggy Melcher.
I see these hills, this house I slip inside.
I see because I watch. Hear because I listen.
I see Revelations number 9. I sing revolutions of time.
I see dumb boys and star friends in a city of dumb angels.
One dumb angel can't speak, another dumb angel can't hear.
And this little piggy went to Hollywood.

Alert and all-hearing, one hundred ears encircle me.
And female flower mouths that tongue desire.

Four Angels, Four Living Beings, will rise.
Faces of men with hair of women, and breastplates of fire.
Their shields glitter guitars with eyes that surround.
Locust and beetles with the sting of scorpions
Prepared for battle, they trumpet broken wings
To domino Reagan and Nixon and the rest to ruin.
One third of heaven's stars are coming down fast
To fall like a red rubber ball of reckoning.

A worm of unbelievable size and length lies on its back.
It is mad, black and hairy, full of sores of pus and poison.
The black man, it says in the White Book,

Will rise to enslave with the arrows of human pollution.
The Great Red Dragon from the Sea and the Woman Clothed in Sun
Will stand on these steps, swim in this pool.
I see the pregnant lady in celestial dimensions.
In agony the Great Red Dragon swims
Beneath to devour the child at birth.
They get to the bottom and stare up at the stars.
And water floods from blue to blood.

But our hole is bottomless to hide in the days of hate.
We seek not pools or treasure.
We dive the void of garbage and re-surface with gold.

Poor deaf angels,
Poor sunk piggies,
Poor ocean dopes.
Dumb angels drown first.

BIRTHDAY

December 4, 1983. 14400 Sunset Boulevard, Pacific Palisades.

"Happy Birthday, Dear Dennis. Happy Birthday to you!"

Dennis blows out the candles. Laughs and jokes with his hosts. Then flips into belligerence.

"C'mon, Hormel. Where is it? Are you gonna deny me on my birthday, dude? Rehab is next week. Everyone gets one last party. Hey, I know about the pantry. I used to live here, you know. Everything that went down. Places to hide."

He pounds the coffee table.

"This was MY HOUSE!"

He zig-zags off the couch into the kitchen.

Yes, he is back in the "log cabin." The same home on Sunset he opened to Charlie and girls 15 years ago. Dennis was drawn here when emotions peaked. It was among the first places he showed Christine McVie during their romance a couple years earlier. During this period, somehow focused, he created *Pacific Ocean Blue*, a solo album of lasting beauty that bared his soul, sandpapered by love and obsession – even as cousin Mike Love deformed the band into Republican rah-rahs, Brian sunk into psychosis, and brother Carl kept them together by the sheer power of his angelic voice.

Now the house was owned by George Hormel, Jr., meat-packing heir and owner of Village Recorders in Westwood. He purchased it long after Dennis had abandoned it to Charlie (letting realtors evict the Family). Hormel was today's reluctant enabler. How could he refuse Dennis? Not on his 39th birthday. Not after 24 hours of:

- Tears
- Bloody knuckles
- Cajoling of co-dependents
- Booze vs. coke vs. the shakes vs. coke vs. booze
- Bashing a car with a baseball bat
- Worst of all – abducting his 15-month-old son.

Early that morning, sleepless, paranoid, he had barged-in on Shawn Love, his barely legal separated wife, in her Santa Monica Bay Inn kitchenette. He found her sleeping with not one but two other dudes, while Dennis-and-Shawn's toddler Gage waddled in the mess. Shawn Love wasn't just another object of love-abuse. She was the daughter of detested Mike Love. Dennis "rescued" Shawn when she was 15 and married her after their son arrived.

By now he had burned through four wives (really five, but one he married twice!) and 10 times that number of luxury cars. Ask anyone who lived near the beach: They'll know someone who got in a crash with Dennis Wilson. He totaled three separate Rolls Royce's owned by Christine McVie. And those were just the accidents. He intentionally torched or bashed the cars of more than one lover.

This marriage was no better.

"What the hell?! Are you fucking crazy?"

- Tossing tables
- Punching walls
- Yanking Shawn in a tug-of-war, with little Gage the prize.

Rip-tiding, clutching each last lover like a life preserver. And now his innocent little boy.

"Child Protective Services will not be happy! You don't like it? Go meditate with your dad!"

He footballed Gage under his arm.

First stop was across the street: An old haunt. Chez Jay steakhouse on Ocean Avenue. Alice the owner unlocked the door to wooly dad and bawling son. Dennis bundled the boy in his jacket and coo'd to him in the tuck-and-roll booth waiting for a taxi and nursing a pint of Popov.

Then, chaos all day as cabbies drove Dennis and little Gage somewhere, anywhere to cool down and change diapers. Dennis had neither home nor car – his license long-ago revoked and finances cut-off by Brother Records. After finding a Venice friend to take Gage, he headed out again.

And by midnight, here he is, back at the Log Cabin, banging through Hormel's kitchen.

"I know every room, Hormy. Every room." In the walk-in pantry he pushes on the polished Craftsman wood. "Lifted to heaven, and sunk to hell. Love and pain... Here we go!"

He slides open the panel revealing a slightly smaller room... and Hormel's vintage wines and liqueurs.

"Denny, why do torture yourself? I mean, I want to help, but this place, for you, it's not healthy. You can't outrun the ghosts."

Dennis snags two bottles of Ketel One. Best stuff he's had in weeks.

"Fuck Shawn Love! Fuck Mike Hate!"

He cranks the cap. But before taking a swig he stares straight into Hormel.

"Love turns to pain, Hormy. You know? Every fucking time."

His eyes pool with tears.

REVERB
December 28, 1983. Basin C–1100, Marina del Rey.

Three weeks after his 39th birthday, on a blue afternoon, at the end of a skinny pier, Dennis stands in his cut-offs. His beard and hair are knotted. Just another Venice burn-out. This is where his yacht Harmony docked before repossession two years prior. Couch surfing has washed him to the Marina, to longtime friend Bill Oster, whose boat is docked next to Harmony's empty slip.

He'd been cursing himself for days. But now, he's upbeat, animated, as if the cloudless air has cleared all remorse, all fear.

"I'm going in again, Bill. Look, I found this picture frame!"

It once contained a wedding photo he had hurled overboard years ago.

"There's more treasure down there!! Look, a string of pearls!"

…

He dives into the dark.

Reverb floods his hearing and a kick-drum sound-checks his heart.

Pump. Pump. Pump. Pump.

From the bottom, the blue – always inside too but faded – now grows and domes the sun. It shimmers into the shape of one pretty saint, one with the eyes of all the women. Then all the women emerge and a whirlpool of faces surge. The circles of their lips overlap and eyes glow round under cascades of hair, then blur back into one. Now she presses closer. She is radiant in total presence. Her breath and pulse sync with his.

Wombed in warmth, in awe of the grace and beauty of her face, he reaches to stroke her cheek. She responds.

An embrace. A smile.

EPILOGUE REMIX

BEACH BOYS VILLANELLE

Diving off a dock of darkened memories
A father with one eye and a son with one ear
He plunged into the drink and never surfaced

It was nearly Dennis not Sharon Tate who Charlie got first
He threw me in the deep end cried Christine McVie
Diving off a dock of darkened memories

Daddy dear never had a hit so he hit his sons
The bad vibes flow from Blue Jay Way to Marina Del Rey
He plunged into the drink and never surfaced

300 pounds of coke-drunk Brian watching "Flipper"
Dad popped-out his glass eye and bared his bloody socket
Diving off a dock of darkened memories

Shattered by acid Brian poured forth masterpieces of pain
His father smacked his ears till he heard in only mono
He plunged into the drink and never surfaced

Dennis drowned in women more than music booze or brothers
A heart forever flooded with blood and love obsessions
Diving off a dock of darkened memories
He plunged into the drink and never surfaced

VIII. Selections from
Fear of Kathy Acker

XXXXXXXXXXXXXX

DEAR MARCI

XXXXXXXXXXXXXX

So what use is emotion? What use is anything? Oh, Oh, I'm not understanding anything anymore, even as perceptions stream in at all angles all hours all pores all doors to the soul in mortal anguish, while nobody is understanding anything. The only question is when to kill oneself.

Not only is there NO ESCAPE FROM PERCEIVING but the only way to deal with pain is to kill oneself. AND NOW YOU ARE THINKING ABOUT SUICIDE, about your sadness that isn't self-pitying, but simply suicidal. I fell in love with your undaunted pessimism. You never wanted any sympathy. Just to be left alone. And your face had this scorched, depleted, devastated, mauled, ragged beauty, which I'll never be able to forget.

Your jagged features are etched in my mind. So are your words: when you said you can't sleep at night because of nightmares of dead fathers and brothers, waving their bloody limbs, and when you said in the morning that you were sick and couldn't get up, and when you talked about your mother. You were a gorgeous manic-depressive and I was just a boy scout, an innocent bystander that wanted to help a soul in trouble when I saw your tear-tracks in the morning, saw this beautiful creature lost in wild bummers and I had to help. I was so struck by this.

Ouch!

I can still see you and hear you and start getting crazy myself and have to divert myself to stop thinking of your gorgeous sad face and how you made me get sick and cry.

As society becomes increasingly depersonalized, and as there are less and less baseball players with nicknames, my chance diminishes for real personal rapport.

Still, I have my desires and my inner life. If no one can ever share these, neither can they take them away.

Meanwhile, you're waking up hungover and suddenly realizing all the failures of last night and your deep depression and there's no escape from the troubles of you and your family and once there were a few victories every now and then in your life, but now it's defeat after defeat and you're only getting older and mostly you're lonely, you're so terribly lonely and just want to die alone.

You walk around, you're not understanding anything. All your day like all your life you're walking around dejected, the school's ugly duckling, then you have an accident and wake up under the plastic surgeon's knife as the most beautiful coed on campus. But when you wake up, you are making out with Ed Asner, and millions of Americans are watching you on TV I am one of those Americans. I hear your dark voice and watch you cock your head. On TV, perceptions stream in like this, no way to deal with the pain. My consciousness is seeping out without my ever having understood what came in. Emotions and baseball games. I'm crying as I watch the commercials.

PUSH YOUR TITTIES TOGETHER. PINCH THE TIPS OF YOUR
TITTIES. I WALK IN THE DOOR.
I AM YOUR TEACHER.
TAKE OFF YOUR SKIRT.
SUCK ME.
RUB YOUR CLIT.
TURN OVER AND SHOW ME YOUR ASSHOLE AND PUSSY
UNDERNEATH.
PLAY WITH YOUR CLIT.
MY HANDS ARE RUBBING YOUR TITS.
MY LIPS ARE TOUCHING YOUR LIPS. MY LIPS ARE YOUR LIPS.
WE ARE CRAWLING IN AND OUT OF EACH OTHER THROUGH OUR
LIPS.
YOU MASTURBATE AND COME HARD.

YOU ARE LETTING LOOSE EVERY KIND OF EMOTION... LOVE IS AN EMOTION.

(And Kathy Acker walks through London rain in scruffy black cowboy boots.)

Then, the UFO.

Even as you know all this is preposterous, it has the cold pinch of reality. It's all happening all over again, just like you're walking down your own street. But when you walk down your street and look up at the cold windy sky that's about to start raining again, you see something new. You see the lights, the beautiful architectonic design of lights on the large flying interconnecting diamonds, dancing harlequin diamonds of light in the sky coming down and silently resting on the street next door to the Champion Auto Parts store. Now a crowd is gathered around, your neighbors and all the shopkeepers and people off the bus. And a hush falls over the crowd as a cool blue throbbing panel slides down invitingly. You long to enter there, and you start to move forward, but you feel the fear and censure of the crowd. All your family and friends. Once you go inside and that thing flies off again, you'll be gone forever. I'll never see you again.

I break into tears right there and they splatter on the sidewalk. The buildings close in around me. I wander home to bed.

```
        X
        X
XXXXXXXXXX
        X
        X
        X
        X
        X
```

'But that didn't really happen'

What really happened is this.

I wake up. Maybe it's all been one of those bad dreams which jerks back to the beginning of itself over and over. Maybe I was never asleep. Maybe I didn't need to sleep to imagine all of this stuff. Maybe I didn't imagine it, maybe it really happened. Or maybe it happened to someone else and I just changed the names around. You tell me. "All writing is cut-up." What post-modernist said that? This question will be on the Midterm. "All reality is a cut-up." What anti-post-modernist said that? This question will be on the Final. Even dreams are a spontaneous collage.

But I remember everything in my life as if it were a dream. And my head is groggy, thick, and throbs inside my bedroom which twirls inside my house. So I get up, waddle into the kitchen to get a glass of orange juice and some Tylenol. Fresh-squeezed orange juice tastes great. I gulp two glasses. I hear some music coming from the living room. I must have left the stereo on. But in the living room everything is off. I DO turn off the stereo, but music keeps playing through the speakers.

"Shit, this is weird!"

And the music itself is pretty weird: like cats meowing through water with bones clinking little boney melodies and flat penises flapping on hot concrete. I don't think this is possible: That I could be hearing this weird music and not be dreaming. I must still be in bed, dreaming that I woke up and drank two glasses of orange juice and turned off the stereo!

So I go back to bed, pull the covers over my head and refuse to hear anything else.

That's when the whispers start. Miniature whispers in my revolving hangover, which puff and hiss before I can actually imagine what they might be saying to me.

"Psssst! We can't hear what you're saying because we're too busy fucking w/ yr mind, ha ha. you are a slimy cock that won't stay hard, ha ha. Listen man you piss shooter bum whore shit. . . . 1/2 of yr life is sorrow and the other 1/2 is dread. . . . ha ha... oh oh! We can't laugh anymore. Now is when we realize that when you finally get the nerve to kill yrself that we'll die too. Yet we can't honestly persuade you not to do it, because what other recourse is there? Yr whole life is one big con game on yr friends who think you are so nice, but the whole time you were scamming on some girl and trying to outmaneuver this guy and all the time trying to get yr name in the gossip pages so that yr wretched life won't have been just a stinky shit that passed down the toilet of oblivion. So don't come crying to us when it's all over and yr hair is gone and you can't see and you've run out of ideas and it's time to quit. We're just a product of yr inability to strain out guilt from all the bullshit you've said. Now the world swirls sickeningly around you and blank inevitability trembles under yr eyelids, right? And you just want somebody to love, but did you actually sacrifice yr self interest for somebody when it counted for them? NO. And now the life flow in yr particular case is about to revert to some other poor uncomprehending id, and yr time is up. SORRY. But you had yr chance to be conscious of the universe while you were here, and all you can think about now is whether you should change the tape on yr answering machine. Forget it. You're not worth the cosmic garbage that went into making you. It's as simple as that.

Good Bye."

All of which means that my ego has slipped out. And this is not the glorious Universe-in-Unity ego-disintegration that Alan Watts talked about. Nor is this a vision of the oversoul, Ergot, who timelessly waits for all humanity to remember itself, piercing the wall of illusion—exploding into Unity. For now I know I'm a human being in this body, but WHO AM I? and who are these people I call my friends? Who is Michelle Clinton? Who were the people that surrounded me at Bob Flanagan's party when I was too stoned on mushrooms? And why were they all pointing at me and laughing? How did I seem to mount the dust mote passing my eyes and ride it into the circling expanding molecules of the living room wall? Or how did I remember such hallucinations when I forget what exactly "I" was/am? Whoever I am I must have a good sense of humor for these people to unhesitatingly poke fun at a poor character who's forgotten who he is. Either that or they're not my friends. What is "my"? What is "me"? I have to get up.

At this point I am trying to force myself awake again, because I see this fat policeman pop up from behind the chair in the corner of my room, and he's got a pistol aimed at my heart and he's squeezing the trigger and out comes that bullet, the gleaming tip streaming silver trails into my chest. Death is like a heavy dark blanket pounding down on my eyes. I can't open them. I can't see. This is all very scary.

Whoa!

What's Napalm?

I climb into my car, head south down the mighty 405, drive to Torrance again, to my old neighborhood, start to relive my childhood shit. I see in my mind the little mudman I unearthed from a corner of the backyard in my lonely afternoon of the living childhood imagination—realler than life, talking to myself as I moved Matchbox cars around a tiny mud and rock freeway system. The little mudman talked to me about bad things in life that I don't want to hear about, about a bad man who pulled down his pants at the girls, and about the nasty neighbors over the high wall who we saw swimming naked in their pool, about a bad boy who stole money from the convent and hopped the wire fence but gashed open his armpit on the steely barbs at the top of the fence, and about being a little mudman who screams when people pull him from the ground, who squirms and dies in little boys' hands when they yank him from the ground, who dies and dissolves back into the earth. And later on my big brothers had brought home 4 orange crawdads from Alondra Park lake and let them loose in the backyard—the dogs got them. Then alone at night in my room I could see the bright red flare from the Torrance Union Carbide chemical plant and refinery. It beamed bright orange right into my room every night.

I asked my dad one day what it was. He told me that's where they make napalm.

"What's napalm?"

"It's a chemical they make, which when it lands on your skin burns and burns and nothing can make it stop burning."

Then I would look at the refinery flare every night and think about people burning and never being able to stop the burning, and nothing can stop the burning, not all the water in the world can stop the burning on your skin and it burns right through your skin and keeps burning, and the refinery flare burns and burns from the refinery, which is like a condensed city with all those lit-up platforms and tiers and towers, and there are all those different refineries scattered around Torrance and Carson and

Compton and Long Beach and San Pedro and they are all like distant orange Ozs seen from the freeway coming home late Sunday night from old Aunt's and Uncle's houses, scary in the night in the back of the '64 Ford Ranch Wagon on the freeway, looking up at the ceiling and seeing the lights and shadows arc and blend on the ceiling of the car as it zooms under streetlamps and bridges.

Last year I asked my dad about the napalm refinery flare and he denied the whole thing, that they ever made napalm there, that he ever told me they did, that he ever told me how it burned and wouldn't stop burning—he denied it all. Maybe he just wiped it from his mind. Maybe he didn't want to admit that he ever told his young son such a horrible thing. Maybe it wasn't my dad.

Praise for Jack Skelley's *Interstellar Theme Park*

Jack Skelley's poems are mind-expanding, vision-inducing, orgasmic, psychedelic drugs, but their poetic beauty is no hallucination. His method: discovering the transcendent in the trivial, the mythic in the mundane. He is a Pop Gnostic who unearths the utopic desire just below the surface of our ultra-mediated culture, hoping to usher in "a Golden Age of pantheistic spasms." Like any realistic revolutionary, he demands the impossible — "I want a planet of toys … jihad of joys … a thick, chewy anarchy in a candy-colored shell." *Interstellar Theme Park* is a funhouse that grants those kinds of wishes and more. Book your trip now!

— Elaine Equi, *The Intangibles*, Coffee House Press

In Skelley's world everything and everyone is volcanic. Cities become backlots; celebrities become saviors. Sharp, always spectacular. One of my very favorite writers on the earth.

— Dennis Cooper

We need Jack Skelley's work now more than ever. Jack's mind on the page helps parse our media-besotted, celebrity-drenched, digitized lives. Whether he's writing a kaleidoscopic erotic prayer to a brand of salad dressing, or making textual bedfellows of Wagner and Betty Rubble, or soulful insider anecdotes from the short life of Rolling Stones founder Brian Jones, or musing tenderly on post-modern fatherhood, Skelley's ability to syncretize pop culture, history, product placement, Catholicism and beyond is a necessary wonder of the contemporary world.

— Amy Gerstler, *An Index of Women*, Penguin Random House

Jack Skelley has been sifting through the detritus of our modern age for 40 years, decoding hidden truths buried deep within our pop icons, media obsessions, consumer culture(s) and other soft delights. As brilliant as the L.A. sun, a singular visionary.

— Lee Ranaldo, American musician, co-founder Sonic Youth

William Blake warned us about the "mind-forg'd manacles" that inhibit the imagination—if only he could be alive today to experience Jack Skelley's writing as it breaks those manacles. Spanning four decades of Skelley's fascination with (and suspicion of) America's society of the spectacle, *Interstellar Theme Park: New and Selected Writing* is a wild ride through the radiant debauchery of contemporary popular culture. Skelley's irresistible poetry and prose take us on a tour of a cosmic, psychosexual playground that features, among others, a mock-epic mocking Elon Musk, a supplication to "Botox Jesus" for the miracle of migraine relief, a Mary Wollstonecraft so "busy inventing goth" that she bequeaths us punk rock, the distorted echo of Meat Puppets guitars heard in a lover's gurgling stomach, twelve Lady Gagas performing "Lady Madonna"—in short, as Skelley writes, all "the levels / of paradise."

— Tony Trigilio, *Ghosts of the Upper Floor*

Jack Skelley's *Interstellar Theme Park* is a Monster. The gravitational pull of its linguistic and other intelligences is so strong, that it's hard to get close without being sucked in. The television is always on and it's always playing America's game, channel switching audaciously through *melopoeia, phanopoeia, logopoeia,* and radiant space. Don't read it unless you've got a ticket to ride through the luminous dimensions of its cosmic ra(n)ge.

— David E. James, *Rock 'N' Film: Cinema's Dance With Popular Music,* Oxford University Press

Despite my dislike of seeing my own name, you're really a good writer — never what's expected.

— Kathy Acker

Jack's Skelley's books include: *Monsters* (Little Caesar Press), *Dennis Wilson and Charlie Manson* (Fred & Barney Press), and *Fear of Kathy Acker* (Semiotext(e)). In addition to many magazines, blogs, etc, Jack's work is widely anthologized. Collections include: *Under 35: The New Generation of American Poets* (ed. Nicholas Christopher, Anchor Books), *Sweet Nothings: An Anthology of Rock and Roll in American Poetry* (ed. Jim Elledge, Indiana University Press), *Coming Attractions* (ed. Dennis Cooper, Little Caesar Press) and *Up Late: American Poetry Since 1970*, (ed. Andrei Codrescu, 4 Walls, 8 Windows).

Jack is an award-winning journalist/editor with 40 years of publishing, from The Atlantic to Salon to Los Angeles Times and Los Angeles Review of Books. He is the former Executive Editor and Associate Publisher of Los Angeles Downtown News. He was editor, publisher & designer of Barney: The Modern Stone-Age Magazine, featuring major artists and writers.

And Jack is songwriter and guitarist for psychedelic surf band Lawndale (SST Records).